ca J. Williams

Pr ons
in sh

r

a presenter

MACMILLAN

Macmillan Education
Between Towns Road, Oxford OX4 3PP
A division of Macmillan Publishers Limited
Companies and representatives throughout the world

ISBN 978-0-230-02876-0

Note to Teachers
Photocopies may be made, for classroom use, of pages 22, 34, 48, 60, 74, 87, 95
and 98 without the prior written permission of Macmillan Publishers Limited.
However, please note that the copyright law, which does not normally permit
multiple copying of published material, applies to the rest of the book.

Designed by Anthony Godber
Illustrated by Kathy Baxendale and Mark Draisey
Cover design by Andrew Oliver
Cover photograph by Getty Images/Stockbyte

Author's acknowledgements
The author wishes to thank César, Dan, Svitlana and Zhan for their enthusiastic
participation and creative contributions.

The publishers would like to thank Adelaide Lane and the team at Tom, Dick
& Debbie Productions for their inspiration and guidance in producing the video
material and Karen Spiller, project manager par excellence, for keeping the whole
thing together.

The publishers would like to thank the following for permission to reproduce their
photographs: Cartoon Stock.com

The authors and publishers are grateful for permission to reprint the following
copyright material: Perseus Books Group for an extract from *Intelligence Reframed*
by Howard Gardner copyright © Basic Books, a member of Perseus Books Group;
Random House Inc and Tilden Press Inc for an extract from *Type Talk at work* by
Otto Kroeger and Janet M Thuesen copyright © 1992 Otto Kroeger and Janet M
Thuesen. Used by permission of Dell Publishing, a division of Random House, Inc
and Tilden Press.

These materials may contain links for third party websites. We have no control over,
and are not responsible for, the contents of such third party websites. Please take
care when accessing them.

Although we have tried to trace and contact copyright holders before publication,
in some cases this has not been possible. If contacted we will be pleased to rectify
any errors or omissions at the earliest opportunity.

Printed and bound in Thailand

2012 2011 2010 2009

10 9 8 7 6 5 4 3

Contents

To the student / presenter

Why *Presentations in English*?

Presentations count. An effective presentation can be the difference between winning or losing a pitch, getting or not getting a job or simply being successful or unsuccessful. The ability to speak English is no guarantee that you can present in English. *Presentations in English* builds and improves your skills and knowledge and gives you the confidence to make effective presentations in English.

Who is the book for?

Learners of English with an intermediate to advanced level of English who need to improve their presentations or will give presentations in their future career.

What does the book include?

- Seven steps: each step includes an introduction and practice of language and skills, presentation analysis, practice of a full presentation, feedback and target setting.
- The video scripts and answer key.
- A DVD with presentations given by four real presenters – not professional actors – who did the training in this book themselves. These non-native speakers of English are Dan, Svitlana, Zhan and César and they had varying experience of presentations before the training. They all prepared and shaped their own presentations on the DVD based on their work experience and the *Presentations in English* training and briefs in this book. You see the journey that Dan, Svitlana, Zhan and César go on. They experiment, have successes, make mistakes, have fun, get anxious and have moments of insight and inspiration – all in all, they're learners just like you.

How is the book organised?

Presentations in English consists of seven steps that build your skills and knowledge from the basics, to examining a whole range of techniques and research. Each step introduces you to new skills and language which you practise. You analyse Dan, Svitlana, Zhan and César's presentations, give a full presentation yourself, get feedback and set targets for your future presentations. The focus is on you at all stages. You are encouraged to examine, analyse, experiment, take a risk, have fun, accept, reject and finally, to find what works for you – to 'find your voice'.

How should I use the book?

Work through the book and DVD step by step. Steps 1–3 give you the basics of presenting, Steps 4–6 build your techniques and Step 7 deals with answering questions in presentations. There is an answer key, but some points and questions are for personal reflection or group discussion and sometimes there is no absolute right or wrong answer. The answers you find are about you 'finding your voice' – an authentic personal style.

General tips

- Try out as many techniques and ideas as you can. Don't reject anything until you've practised it.
- Give yourself plenty of time for analysis, personal feedback and setting targets.
- Film yourself making your presentations. You may get points for improvement on film that you may not get in other types of feedback.
- Record your targets, as written targets get better results.

To the trainer

What is *Presentations in English*?

Presentations in English is a complete course in presenting in English that consists of:

- Seven steps: each step includes an introduction and practice of language and skills, presentation analysis, practice of a full presentation, feedback and target setting.
- The video scripts and answer key.
- A DVD with presentations given by four non-native speakers who did the training in this book. They aren't professional actors but learners who prepared all the presentations on the DVD themselves, based on their work experience and the training and briefs in the book. Please note they sometimes make mistakes in English.

Why *Presentations in English* for presenting in English?

Some estimates say that over 30 million presentations are given every day. Many of these presentations are given in English by non-native speakers. Many are given badly as presenters often don't know how to go about structuring and shaping a presentation or how to use English to maximum effect during a presentation. Presenters need a skill set and a level of professionalism and confidence that means they can do much more than just 'get by'. This book takes a step-by-step approach to developing presentation skills and encourages presenters to find their own authentic style for presenting.

How can you use *Presentations in English*?

- There are seven steps in the book. If you have a short course or a one or two day seminar, the basics of presenting are covered in Steps 1–3. Steps 4–6 cover a variety of techniques and research and Step 7 deals with interactive presentations question and answer sessions. It is advisable to work progressively through the steps although Step 7 could be handled as a separate unit.
- Many questions require personal reflection and group discussion. Sometimes there are no definitive answers as presenters are taken on a journey where they find their own voice for presenting in English.
- You should film the full presentations for feedback sessions, if possible. This allows learners to get a view of how others see them and they may pick up points that might not be recognised otherwise. If you are working with a group, encourage the group to give feedback on their colleagues' performances and if you are doing one-to-one coaching, encourage the presenter to analyse his or her own performance. This is part of the process where presenters learn to find what they like and don't like in presentations.
- Always allow presenters the necessary scope and time for experimentation, (subjective) analysis, feedback and personal target setting as the emphasis is on presenters developing an authentic style and approach that fits and reflects their personality, line of business and level of English. Authentic presenters are congruent: their voices, language and bodies are in harmony with the message they are giving. Help your learners to find this authentic voice.

Introduction

A Watch the interviews with the four presenters at the beginning of their course and answer the questions.

🔘 0.01 **Dan**

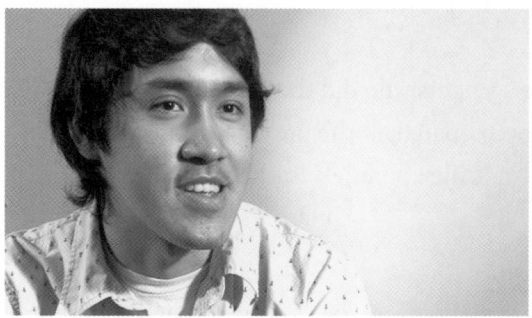

1 What does Dan do?
2 Where is he from?
3 Why is he doing the presentations training?
4 How does he describe the differences between presenting in English and in Thai?
5 What targets has he got?

🔘 0.02 **Svitlana**

1 Where is Svitlana from?
2 What is she doing at the moment?
3 Why is she doing the presentations training?
4 What problems has she got with presenting in English?
5 What targets has she got?

🔘 0.03 **Zhan**

1 Where is Zhan from?
2 What does he do?
3 Why is presenting in English important to his work?

🔘 0.04 **César**

1 Where is César from?
2 What does he do?
3 Why is he doing the presentations training?
4 What targets has he got?
5 What problems has he got with presenting in English?

Presentations diary

B It's a good idea to keep a diary during the *Presentations in English* course. Start your diary by writing about the points below.

1 Write three reasons why presentations are important in your job, your area of business or your studies.
2 Write three things you like about presenting.
3 Write three reasons why presenting in English is problematic for you.
4 Write five targets for yourself in presenting in English.

Step 1 Lay solid foundations

1 The start

Attention curve

A Look at this graph. The vertical axis represents the attention of the audience and the horizontal axis shows time during an average presentation. How would you draw a curve in this graph?

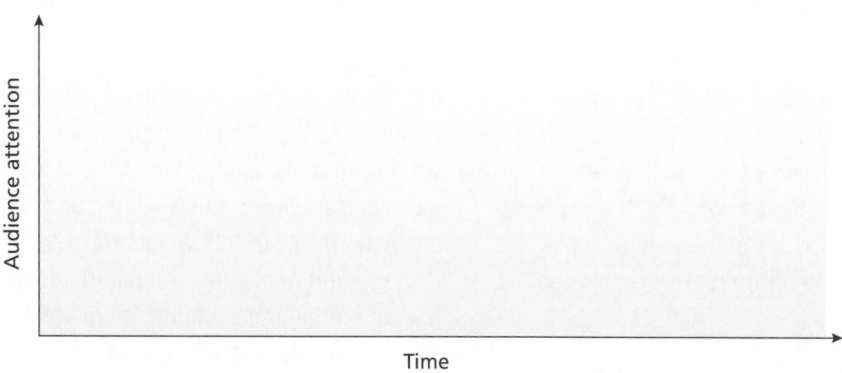

B Now, look at the graph in the answer key on page 100. At which points in a presentation can the audience most easily remember what the presenter says?

Who, why, what, how

A Look at the audience's questions (1–8) and match the numbers with the type of information.

Who is the presenter? ....

Why are we all here? ....

What is he going to talk about? ....

How is he going to organise the presentation? ....

The presentation **journey**

Giving a presentation is like taking your audience from start to finish on a journey. At the start, your audience require some basic information before they can accompany you on this journey. Once they have the information, they're on your side, attentive and ready to listen to every step of the journey along to your final message.

Who

Introduce yourself. Clearly, the amount of information you give about yourself and your work and the level of formality you use, depends on the presentation you're giving. For example, for a presentation to a group of your colleagues, you probably don't need to give your name and background and you can use informal language. A presentation to a new client can require more detailed information about your background and experience and a more formal approach. Make sure that you're comfortable talking about your past and present experience in such cases.

Why

Tell your audience your destination – the reason they're there to listen to you and the purpose of your presentation. If the audience don't know why they should listen, they won't have any reason to accompany you along your journey. The 'why' is linked to the conclusion, your final message – probably, the most important part of your presentation.

What

Outline the roadmap – the main points that you're going to develop and the order in which you would like to develop these. When your audience have a clear view of the roadmap you want to navigate, they can follow you more easily and can also see you're planned, prepared and effectively managing the presentation. There are good reasons for giving the roadmaps, as research shows your audience listen better and remember better and more when they know the structure and shape of your presentation. The technique we use to give the roadmap is called 'sequencing'. This is a very simple technique as it just involves using language such as *one, two, three* or *firstly, secondly, thirdly*. Nevertheless, it is also highly effective as 'sequencing' or 'ordering', as it is sometimes called, is a principle of memory by which we recall information.

How

Put yourself into your audience's shoes: address your audience's needs. Your audience won't listen to you as you go into the main part of your presentation if they have other concerns. They may be thinking: *How long do I have to sit here? Do I have to take notes? When can I ask questions? Is there any coffee here?* It can therefore be useful to answer such questions in your 'start' so that your audience are ready to listen.

Your 'start' should include these points but at the same time not be too long. Ninety seconds is a good guideline as there's evidence that you begin to lose listeners after this amount of time. Your audience tend to listen to your every word and form an impression of you in these ninety seconds. An accurate 'start' helps to create a good impression and you should aim to be grammatically accurate at this stage.

C Read through these phrases. Write 'who', 'why', 'what' or 'how' next to each phrase. Check any vocabulary you don't know.

1 On behalf of Mr Keane, may I welcome you to Jackson Inc. My name's Jo Black and I'm responsible for … ....

2 My purpose today is to … ....

3 I'm going to develop three main points. First, … Second, … Third, … ....

4 Let me introduce myself. I am … I am a … ....

5 I'll pass round copies of my slides so you can make notes as I go through the presentation. ....

6 Before I continue, let me tell you something about myself. ....

7 Today I would like to give you a general overview of … ....

8 I've divided my presentation into three main points. I would like to begin with … ....

9 So, I'll be addressing three main points and the first one is going to be … The second point will be … And finally the last point is … ....

10 I'm going to outline three proposals. Firstly, I'll … Then, I'd like to … and finally … ....

11 Today, I'm going to bring you up to date with … ....

12 The presentation should last about five minutes. ....

13 We'll take a short coffee break at about 10.30. ....

14 My objective today is to … ....

15 Morning everyone. Thanks for coming. My name is Luca and I'm in charge of … ....

16 If you have any questions, I'd be grateful if you could leave them until the end. ....

17 I'm happy to take any questions after that. ....

18 For those who don't know me, my name is Carlos López and I'm the managing director. ....

19 We can take two or three questions at the end of each point. ....

20 You don't need to take notes as we'll be handing out presentation booklets. ....

21 I would like to start with … And then … Lastly … ....

22 Today, I'm going to tell you … ....

23 What I am going to do today is review … ....

24 Please feel free to interrupt me at any time if you have a question. ....

25 The reason we are here today is to … ....

26 Morning everyone. I'm … I'm a … at … ....

D 🔘 1.01, 1.02 Watch César and Zhan's 'starts' to their Step 1 presentations and tick the phrases they used.

Find Your Voice

Don't learn all these phrases now. Highlight one or two from each category that you really like or think are useful for you. Learn them by using them in your presentation practice – prepare the 'start' of a presentation that is typical of your work situation, using the phrases you wish to learn. When you're ready, stand up and present your 'start'.

Grammar

A 🔲 1.03, 1.04 **Watch Dan and Svitlana's 'starts' to their Step 1 presentations. Complete the phrases they used to give the 'whats' of their presentations.**

Dan

1 Firstly, I .... some general info …

2 Then, I .... to the economy …

3 … and then I .... go into details …

Svitlana

4 Today I .... tell you why …

5 I .... by telling you what …

6 I .... to giving you a few examples.

1 What forms do they use?

2 Why do you think it's a good idea to use a variety of forms?

'will'

Form
will / shall + infinitive (without *to*) *Firstly, **I'll go** through the background to the project.* *I **will finish** by outlining the changes we made to the original schedule.*

- *Shall* is much less common than *will* in British English and hardly ever used in American English.
- *Will* is a modal auxiliary verb and doesn't add *-s* in the third person singular.
- We usually use the contracted form in speaking:
  *Firstly **I'll look** at …*

'be going to'

Form
be going to + infinitive *Today **I'm going to** tell you why I chose this topic and how you will benefit from my research.* ***I'm going to** tell you a little bit about my research.*

Note

It is advisable not to overuse one form at the start of a presentation. We can use both *will* and *be going to* to give the 'why' and / or 'what' of a presentation. *Will* is used here to give future information and *be going to* is used to indicate a plan. Note that we don't normally use *will* to talk about future events which are already decided or planned.

- *Going to* can be pronounced as *gonna* in informal speech. This is much more common in American English. In British English, it can sound informal.

'would ('d) like to'

Form
would like ('d like) to + infinitive   **I'd like to move** *on to a comparison of last and this year.*   *I* **would like to give** *you an overview of trademark law.*

- We use *would like to* at the beginning of a presentation to politely state what we want to do.
- Avoid using more direct forms, e.g. *I want* at this stage of a presentation. Use these at later stages.

B **Here are the 'whats' from three presentations. Change the overuse of *will* to create more varied and interesting 'whats'.**

1 Firstly, I'll give the background to the project. Then, I'll tell you about the present situation and then I'll show the future changes.

2 My first point will be to show you the structure of the department, my second point will be our work procedures and my third point will be suggestions for greater efficiency.

3 I'll develop three main points. Firstly, I'll give a general overview. Second, I'll move on to specifics and third, I'll describe the overall changes.

Find Your Voice

Now look again at the 'start' you presented on page 11. Have you used a good variety of forms in the 'what' section? Revise your 'start'. If you want, present your 'start' again.

2 The finish

Signal, summary, conclusion, closing remarks

A   Read the text about the 'finish' of a presentation and answer the questions below.

Make your final message clear

Henry trained himself in the 'dramatic pause'.

Stay in control until the very last second and follow these steps at the 'finish' of your presentation.

Firstly, pause briefly and **signal** clearly that you are now ready to finish the presentation. The audience will start to listen again closely at this point.

Then, make your **summary**, giving a brief overview of what has already been said. The summary is a reflection of your 'what' and looks back. It should not be too long as you will lose your audience's attention again, but detailed enough to cover your points. This can be a difficult balance to achieve! A good summary gives your listeners time to reflect on the content and builds up to your conclusion, making your conclusion stronger, more powerful and more effective. A conclusion without a summary can sound incomplete as your audience may not have listened to every point during the main part of the presentation and the purpose can be lost. Avoid giving any conclusions while you are making your summary.

After this, give your **conclusion**. This is a reflection of your 'why' and looks forward to what you want people to do or think after your presentation. It should follow logically from your summary. There are different kinds of conclusions: you can make a call for action, make a recommendation or assure your audience that they're better informed. This is the destination of your journey and the most important part of your presentation.

Finally, make your **closing remarks** by thanking your audience, asking for questions or passing round your presentation handouts.

1   Why don't some people finish their presentations effectively in your opinion?
2   Do you agree that every presentation has some kind of conclusion?
3   Have you ever thought 'What was the point?' after listening to a presentation?

B   Write *Sig* (Signal), *Sum* (Summary), *Conc* (Conclusion) or *CR* (Closing Remarks) next to the phrases below.

1   So, that brings me to the end of my presentation. ....
2   Let me summarise what we've looked at. ....
3   Thank you for your attention. ....
4   I'll briefly summarise the main issues. ....
5   I'll now hand out … ....
6   I suggest Johannes … and Michel … ....
7   I'd like to summarise. ....
8   I'd like to conclude by strongly recommending … ....
9   So, that completes our presentation. ....
10   Let me just go over the key points again. ....
11   To sum up … ....
12   I trust you gained an insight into … ....
13   To conclude, I'd like to leave you with the following thought … ....
14   Well, that covers everything I want to say. ....
15   If you have any questions, I'd be happy to answer them. ....
16   At this stage, I'd like to go over … ....
17   In my opinion, the only way forward is to … ....
18   Thank you for listening. ....
19   To summarise, I'll run through my three topics. ....
20   In conclusion, I'd like to leave you with the following idea. ....

Find Your Voice

Highlight the phrases above that you really like or think are useful for you, keeping in mind the kinds of conclusion that you often have to make in your presentations. Do you …

- make recommendations?
- give information?
- motivate?
- inspire?
- give a call to action?
- persuade?

Grammar

A 🔵 **1.05 Watch the summary from the 'finish' to César's Step 1 presentation. Answer the questions.**

1 What tense did César use in his summary?

2 Do you think this tense is effective when giving a summary? Why?

3 Did César follow the recommended procedure in his 'finish'?

4 Was this effective?

Present perfect

Form
have / has + past participle **I've told** *you about the current situation, the problems and the solutions.*

- In general we use the present perfect to connect the past with the present. The action may be complete, but the time period is either not finished or definite.

  So, as we **have seen** *today, there are very good reasons to …*

- Compare with the past simple where the time period is finished and definite.

  So, as we **saw** *last week, there are very good reasons to …*

B **Complete this presentation extract with the present perfect or simple past form of the verbs.**

Let's now turn to training. Many other international companies (1) .... (envy) our development programme five years ago. But, the internal situation (2) .... (be) actually far from satisfactory. Then, each department (3) .... (make) its own decisions, (4) .... (set) its own budget and (5) .... (appoint) its own trainers. This often (6) .... (mean) that staff (7) .... (not attend) training that (8) .... (be) necessary for their jobs. We (9) .... (waste) both time and money. All in all, we (10) .... (not have) the best possible solution. How (11) .... we .... (change) things since then? Well, all training measures (12) .... (be) centralised. This year, we (13) .... (make) HR responsible for all decisions on training. We (14) .... (allocate) one central budget and (15) .... (introduce) one integrated system. Training (16) .... (become) much more effective and targeted. We (17) .... (start) to build modern training facilities and you are sitting today in our brand new purpose built Academy. I'm sure that you must agree that today we (18) .... (find) a much better, more effective and targeted solution than the one we (19) .... (have) before. I'll just quickly summarise what we (20) .... (see) so far.

> **Find Your Voice**
>
> Now prepare and present the 'finish' of a presentation, typical of your work or study situation.
>
> - Include any phrases you want to learn.
> - Use the present perfect in your summary.
> - Make sure you give a clear logical conclusion.

3 Structuring

Signposting

A 🔘 **1.06** Watch an extract from an interview with Dan after his Step 1 presentation.

1   How does structuring a presentation help Dan?

2   Do you agree with his comments?

B 🔘 **1.07, 1.08** Phrases 1–22 below are examples of signposts. Read them and check any vocabulary you don't know. Now, watch the main content of Svitlana and Zhan's Step 1 presentations and tick the signposts they use.

1   Moving on now to … ………

2   I would like to begin by … ………

3   Let's now turn to … ………

4   Let's start with my presentation. ………

5   So, first of all … ………

6   Now, turning to … ………

7   Now, what about …? ………

8   Let me move on to … ………

9   So, that's the general picture for … ………

10 I'd like to conclude this point by saying … ………

11 This leads me to a point … ………

12 So, we've looked at … ………

13 That completes my overview of … ………

14 Let's just recap … ………

15 So, that's pretty much … ………

16 and this is … ………

17 Next we come to … ………

18 So, that was … ………

19 My next point is … ………

20 That's all I want to say about … ………

21 So, that covers this point. ………

22 And finally … ………

C Look at the graph and read the text below. Why are signposts important?

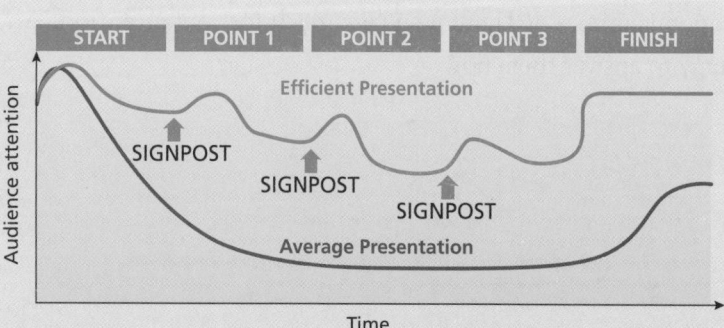

How do signposts work?

Signposting helps you structure and shape the main content of your presentation. Signposts create 'verbal paragraphs' or 'verbal signals' and raise the attention curve at the beginning and end of each point of your presentation. The technique allows you to guide the audience through the structure of your presentation linking one point to the next. The audience can't see your notes and can't look forward to see what is coming. You know where you're going on your journey and you need to guide your audience by telling them exactly where you are on the roadmap of your presentation. This is a simple but highly effective technique that adds clarity to your presentations.

Delivery

Pausing

A 🔘 1.09 **Watch an extract from an interview with Svitlana after her Step 1 presentation. How does pausing help the audience?**

B 🔘 1.10 **Watch an extract from an interview with César after his Step 1 presentation.**

1 Which additional techniques did César mention?
2 What are the benefits of these techniques for a non-native speaker?
3 Can you think of any additional advantages?
4 Why do you think pausing sometimes feels uncomfortable for a presenter?

C **Read the text about pausing and then practise saying Svitlana's text below with pauses.**

> Pause before using the signpost to turn to a new point. Count up to ten in your head and breathe deeply. This helps your audience to assimilate your information and gives you the chance to control your nerves.

That is why identifying the kinds of deviations and studying them is a necessary step in building a more just and successful society. // To summarise, // I will run through my three main points. // Firstly, I would like to emphasise one more time the importance of studying a deviant behaviour of economic agents as a separate subject. // Secondly, I would like to bring your attention to the importance of researching the origins of economic crimes // and thirdly, we need to be aware of different kinds of deviations and to try to convert negative deviations into positive ones whenever possible. // In conclusion, I'd like to leave you with the idea that it is up to you to improve the quality of your lives and societies you live in by realising that you can deal with a deviant behaviour efficiently by simply avoiding participating in economic crimes. // Thank you very much for your attention. And, if you have any questions, I will be happy to answer them now.

Find Your Voice

Get into groups of five. If your group has fewer than five people, one person can take two or more roles. Role play a presentation using the structure below.

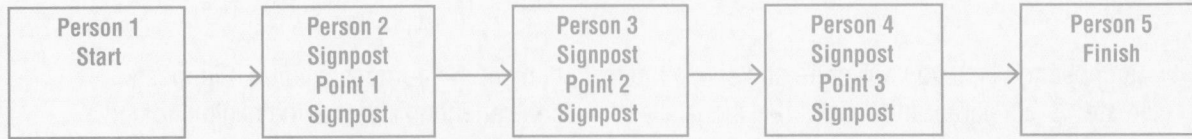

Person 1 Start	Person 2 Signpost Point 1 Signpost	Person 3 Signpost Point 2 Signpost	Person 4 Signpost Point 3 Signpost	Person 5 Finish

Keep it short and simple (KISS). Concentrate on using the language and techniques you have learned so far in this step for starting, finishing and signposting. Change roles for different presentations.

Suggestions for presentation topics:

- three countries for a good holiday
- three cars
- three great films or books
- three restaurants in your city

4 Full presentation

Analysis

A   🔘 1.11 Read the brief for the Step 1 presentation on page 21. Then, watch César's short Step 1 presentation and look at the feedback from a member of César's audience. Which comments do you agree with?

Feedback form: Lay solid foundations					
	Poor	OK	Yes!	Wow!	Comments
Start			X		Seems to be very friendly and is not too nervous.
Who				X	
Why			X		Good pausing – I like the use of the flip chart here.
What			X		
How	X				Doesn't do this.
Variety			X		
Signposting			X		Clear at the beginning of points, but more signposting at the end of the points. 'Let me just turn to', 'This brings me to my 3rd point' – good variety.
Pausing		X			Needs more pausing between some of the points.
Organisation			X		Simple, but clear. Don't like all the interaction with the flip chart.
Finish				X	There could have been a clearer signal between the last point and the 'finish'. Difference between summary and conclusion was very clear. It works even though it's a short presentation.
Signal			X		
Summary				X	
Present perfect				X	
Conclusion				X	
Closing remarks		X			

B 📀 1.11 Analysis and discussion help you to 'find your voice' for your own presentations. Watch César's presentation again. As you watch, rate his performance in the Feedback form yourself. Remember that analysis is subjective and you don't have to agree with the assessment in **A**. If you are working together with a group, discuss your analysis with the group after the presentation.

Feedback form: Lay solid foundations					
	Poor	**OK**	**Yes!**	**Wow!**	**Comments**
Start Who Why What How Variety					
Signposting					
Pausing					
Organisation					
Finish Signal Summary Present perfect Conclusion Closing remarks					

Preparation and presentation

A   Read the brief and prepare your own presentation. Don't forget to KISS (Keep it Short and Simple)!

Full presentation practice: Giving information

Subject and structure

Choose from the following list or think of your own subject.

- My department and / or my company
- My industry
- My university
- My research
- My country

Take any direction you wish with your chosen subject, but divide your presentation into three clear parts using the structure below.

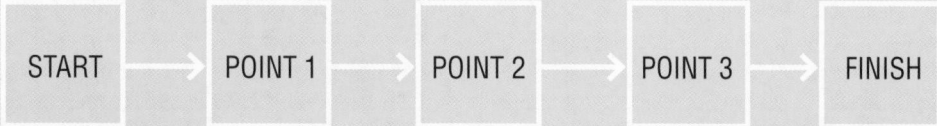

Your audience

You are making this presentation to a group of people who are very important for your future career. This could be your board of directors, a group of external professors, an assessment centre panel or an audience at an international conference, for example. Describe your audience before you start your presentation.

Your targets

- To have a fluent 'who', 'why', 'what', 'how' start
- To have a well-structured and signposted presentation
- To finish well with a summary and clear conclusion
- To leave a good impression by giving a well-prepared presentation

B   Give your full presentation.

Feedback and targets

A   If you're working in a group, analyse each others' presentations, using the Feedback form below. If you're working alone, record yourself and analyse your own performance.

Feedback form: Lay solid foundations					
	Poor	OK	Yes!	Wow!	Comments
Start Who Why What How Variety					
Signposting					
Pausing					
Organisation					
Finish Signal Summary Present perfect Conclusion Closing remarks					

Presentations diary

B   Look back at your feedback on your Step 1 presentation and, if possible, watch your presentation again. Now read 1–4 below and write your diary for Step 1.

1   What was positive for you? List three aspects.

2   Identify one thing you could improve.

3   Identify one thing that didn't work at all for you.

4   Set yourself two targets for your next full presentation.

Step 2 Connect with your audience

1 Jump start

Introduction

A Discuss these questions.

1 What do you think 'jump start' means?

2 Why do you think a 'jump start' is effective? Can you think of any examples of a 'jump start'?

B Read this text. Write the techniques from the box below in gaps (1–7) in the text.

> What's in it for me? (WIIFM)   Question and answer   Expert testimony or historical evidence
> Quotations   Meet the people   Shocking statement or startling statistic   Enrolment questions

Hot tips to 'jump start' your presentation

(1) ....

Make your audience feel welcome as they arrive. Smile, make introductions, say a few words about yourself and ask some questions. Offer some refreshments. This technique helps to:
* break the ice
* calm your nerves
* build a relationship
* initiate dialogue
* create interaction

GOOD FOR: Presentations to small groups

(2) ....

Address the audience's needs and concerns by telling them what benefits they will gain from listening to your presentation and use the word 'you' when you do this. This technique helps to:
* focus on the needs of your audience
* focus on benefits and not features
* create desire and anticipation
* raise expectations
* build rapport

GOOD FOR: Sales pitches or presentations where you need to persuade or convince

(3) ....

Question the audience directly and get them to respond to you by answering 'yes' or 'no' or by raising hands. This technique helps to:
* focus the audience on the subject
* generate an interactive relationship
* create dialogue
* build interest

GOOD FOR: Small to medium-sized audiences

(4) ....

Find something original or exciting in newspapers, magazines, books, in-house literature, press releases or on the Internet. Make it clear that you are using somebody else's words. This technique helps to:
* give another voice
* create interest
* build credibility

GOOD FOR: All types of presentation

(5) ....

Say something which is short and simple but unusual, surprising and / or provocative. Clarify your source. This technique helps to:
* get a high level of attention with a shock effect
* give another voice

GOOD FOR: Most presentations but take care the shock effect does not alienate the audience

(6) ....

Give objective evidence or facts from an authoritative source. This technique helps to:
* give another voice
* build credibility
* be convincing

GOOD FOR: Specialist presentations

(7) ....

Ask something and then go on to answer it yourself. This technique helps to:
* raise expectations
* engage the audience in problem-solving thinking
* make the audience want to see 'what's on the next page'

GOOD FOR: Presenting recommendations / solutions

C **Now match examples of jump starts (a–g) below with the techniques 1–7.**

1 What's in it for me? (WIIFM) ....

2 Question and answer ....

3 Expert testimony or historical evidence ....

4 Quotations ....

5 Meet the people ....

6 Shocking statement or startling statistic ....

7 Enrolment questions ....

a The benefit to you is that you will have a better product that will do a better job.

b In today's newspaper, our CEO stated 'The Internet is the aggressive revolutionary army of our age. It will kill our children' and I'm going to show you why we need to rationalise our business before we lose it completely.

c We often talk about creativity and promoting a culture of creativity. But what do we mean exactly? I'm sure each of you would give a different answer. So, I'm here today to answer this question and explain exactly what we mean when we say 'creativity' in our company.

d Hi my name's Laura Schmidt. Please help yourself to coffee or tea while we're waiting for everyone to arrive.

e I'm holding the latest government health report in my hands. It states that the chance of getting some cancers has actually risen from one in twelve to one in nine in the last few years. The report goes on to link this to household products and says that more than 500 – more than 500 – manufactured chemicals found in the everyday environment are believed to mimic and disrupt hormones. Today, I'm going to examine what this means for us in our business sector.

f How many of you have pitched for new business and failed to get it? How many of you here hate giving presentations? How many of you think your presentations are boring and uninspiring? Raise your hands. Thanks. Well, this afternoon we will be exploring …

g Young girls between the ages of nine and fourteen stated that their number one fear is getting fat. They're more afraid of becoming fat than they are of nuclear war, climate change or losing their parents. Our new wellness product range is all about sensible diet and changing attitudes and what I'd like to do is …

Techniques

Meet the people

A Get into small groups.

Presenter
- Greet the other members of the group as they come into the room.
- Walk to the front of the room and make your Step 1 presentation 'start' again.

Rest of group
- Come into the room on your own or with another member of the group.
- Sit down and watch the 'start' of the presenter's Step 1 presentation again.

Change roles and do the activity again.

Discuss these questions.
1 How did 'meeting the people' help you as a presenter?
2 How did 'meeting the people' help you as a member of the audience?

WIIFM

B Look at these two examples of WIIFM.
1 *We'll take a look at health and safety. If you know the procedures, you'll know exactly what to do in the case of an accident or emergency here in the company.*
2 *We'll take a look at health and safety. This is important to you because you need to know something about legal requirements when you deliver to the chemical industry.*

What audience do you think each is targeted at?
a suppliers
b customers
c employees
d delegates at an international conference

Look at the 'why' sentences (1–3) below.
1 What I would like to do is give you an overview of the restructuring programme.
2 My goal in this presentation is to give you three alternatives for marketing strategy.
3 It is our intention to fill you in on our latest product portfolio.

Choose one audience (a–d) above and prepare a follow-on WIIFM sentence for each 'why' sentence (1–3). Use the phrases below to help you.

This is important to you because …	*What you will gain from this is …*
I am telling you this because …	*The benefit to you is …*
The reason you need to hear this …	*If you …, you'll …*

Present your three WIIFMs. Can the rest of the group identify your target audience?

Quotations

C   2.01 **Watch the 'start' of Svitlana's presentation of the Orange Revolution in Ukraine to the Oxford Ukrainian Society and answer the questions below.**

1 Have you ever heard quotations used in a presentation before?

2 Do you find her use of this technique effective?

Read the quotations below.

'Quality is remembered long after the price is forgotten.' *Gucci*

'The harder you work, the luckier you get.' *Gary Player*

'I have the simplest tastes. I am always satisfied with the best.' *Oscar Wilde*

Choose one of the quotations and build it into the 'start' you presented in Step 1. Stand up and present your 'start'.

Now, find an original quotation about your organisation or a quotation that was given by somebody from your organisation. Build this into a full presentation 'start'. Present this.

Discuss these questions.

1 Do you find the first or the second 'start' more effective?

2 Why do you find this 'start' more effective?

3 What in-house resources can you use in your organisation to find original quotations?

4 Do you think it is possible to make up a quotation or change a quotation?

Shocking statement or startling statistic

D 🔊 2.02 The audience for César's Step 2 presentation were his peers – academics and trademark practitioners. Listen to César's comments about this 'start' and answer the questions below.
1 What does he say about his opening statement?
2 What did he say the reaction of his peers would be to this statement?

🔊 2.03 Watch an extract from César's 'start' to his Step 2 presentation. What was his shocking statement?

Find a shocking statement or startling statistic that relates explicitly to the 'why' of the 'start' you gave in Step 1. Build this statement into your 'start' and present it.

Combining 'jump start' techniques

E 🔊 2.04, 2.05 Dan and Zhan used a combination of 'jump start' techniques in the 'start' of their Step 2 presentations. Watch the presentation extracts and identify the techniques in the table below.

Technique	Dan	Zhan
Audience	*Small group at a seminar on independent bookshops*	*Group of arts undergraduates wanting to learn more about science*
Meet the people		
WIIFM		
Quotations		
Shocking statement or startling statistic		
Expert testimony or historical evidence		
Enrolment questions		
Question and answer		

Dan and Zhan used three more techniques. Watch the extracts again. What are they?

> **Find Your Voice**
>
> Using a combination of 'jump start' techniques is simple and very effective. Revise your Step 1 'start' and include a combination of 'jump start' techniques. Now present your 'start'.

Grammar

Future continuous

Form
will / shall + be + -ing   I **will / shall be** telling you about the past performance.   We **will / shall be** informing you about the future alternatives.

- There is no difference in meaning between *shall* and *will* here. *Shall* is much less common than *will* in British English and hardly ever used in American English.
- We use the future continuous to refer to future events which are fixed and part of a planned sequence.
- You can use this tense at the 'start' of your presentations to give your structure and intentions. *So, in my presentation today I'll be outlining three proposals. Firstly, I'll be talking about the prospects for the XYZ product and then I'll be moving on to my second point. Lastly, …*
- We usually use the contracted form in speaking. *I'll be talking about …*

A   **Complete this 'start' using the future continuous of the verbs in brackets.**

So, in my presentation today I (1) .... (bring) you up to date with the Bluebrick project. First, I (2) .... (look) at the background to the project. Then, I (3) .... (examine) current activities and finally, I (4) .... (outline) future prospects.

B   **Complete this 'start' using the correct tenses of the verbs in brackets. Use the future continuous where appropriate.**

This morning we (1) .... (present) the new design. The reason you (2) .... (need) to hear this is that it's important to bring your design into the 21st century. We (3) .... (like) to show you the recommendations from both the external design consultancy and from your own internal departments, and finally we (4) .... (show) you how we can bring this to market in just six months.

> **Find Your Voice**
>
> Look at the brief for the Step 2 presentation on page 33. Prepare a 'start' for this presentation including the use of the future continuous. Read the 'start' to yourself until you begin to feel you are using the future continuous naturally. Build at least one future continuous into your presentation 'starts'.

2 Finish with a bang

Introduction

A Read the comments (1–5) below about presentations that 'finished with a bang'. Then answer the questions.

1 The presenter put a big cardboard box on the table at the start of the presentation and at the end he said, 'I guess you've all been wondering what this box is.' And we all had …! The conclusion was to think 'outside the box'. Then, the presenter took a hammer, smashed the box and threw it in the rubbish bin. It was dramatic and it 'hammered home' the message.

2 The presentation had been about stress at work and the presenter read some paragraphs from Joseph Heller's novel, *Something Happened*. Everybody was laughing but there was a serious message as the novel extract illustrated the point of the presentation exactly.

3 One presenter gave a talk about creativity. At the end she played some music and got everyone involved, clapping to the music. She danced across the stage. I'll never forget it because it was different. It really gave the presentation impact. I've often played music in my office since.

4 He ended with a quote from our CEO that underlined what he had said about the problems in our company. He delivered it with real power and conviction and I can still remember it today.

5 The presenter gave a very effective, well-organised presentation. Then, he did a little something extra and informed us there was a gift underneath our chairs. There was a package taped underneath every chair and inside we found a T-shirt with the new logo and samples of the product from the presentation. It was a surprise for everyone and I still have the T-shirt!

1 What are the features of a 'finish with a bang' according to the comments above?
2 Can you add any 'finish with a bang' techniques?

B 2.06 Watch Svitlana's summary from her Step 2 presentation and answer the questions.
1 What technique did she use and was it relevant to the presentation?
2 Did she deliver her summary with power and conviction?

C 2.07 Now watch Zhan's 'finish' to his Step 2 presentation and answer the questions.
1 What technique(s) did he use and was the 'bang' relevant to the presentation?
2 Did he 'hammer home' the message?

> **Find Your Voice**
>
> Revise your Step 1 'finish' and include a 'finish with a bang'. Now present your 'finish'.

Delivery

Verbal garbage

A 💿 2.08 **Watch part of Dan's Step 1 presentation and answer the questions.**
1 Which filling phrase did he use most often?
2 What is the effect of using this phrase so often?
3 How many times did Dan use the filling phrase?

B 💿 2.09 **Dan got feedback on his Step 1 presentation and watched some of his own performance. He set himself the target of eliminating some of his verbal garbage.**

Watch part of Dan's new Step 2 presentation and answer these questions.
1 How many times did Dan use the filling phrase in this extract?
2 Did Dan achieve his target?

C **Do you have any verbal garbage? Watch your Step 1 presentation or ask colleagues for feedback.**

Final consonant

D 💿 2.10 **Watch two versions from Svitlana's conclusion to her Step 2 presentation. Answer the questions.**
1 Which word was pronounced differently in the first and second versions?
2 How did Svitlana pronounce the word to give the 'wrong meaning' in the first version?
3 What effect did this have on her final conclusion?
4 How did she pronounce the word to give the 'right meaning' in the second version?

E **Read these sentences aloud. Pronounce the final consonant in the underlined words and pause before reading the next word.**
1 Employees must see we are <u>reacting</u> sensitively.
2 We'll have problems if they think we are not <u>supporting</u> humane conditions.
3 It is only by <u>buying</u> efficient equipment that we will remain competitive.
4 <u>Demonstrating</u> attention to detail will win the client over.
5 <u>Broadcasting</u> offensive commercials is not the answer at all.

Find Your Voice

Read the brief for the full presentation in Step 2 on page 33. Decide on your presentation and prepare a 'start' and 'finish', using the 'jump start' and 'finish with a bang' techniques. Don't forget to lay solid foundations! Present the 'start' and 'finish'.

---

4 Full presentation

Analysis

A  2.11 Watch César's full Step 2 presentation to academics and trademark practitioners. As you watch, rate the points in the Feedback form below. If you are working together with a group, discuss your analysis with the group.

Feedback form: Connect with your audience					
	Poor	OK	Good	Wow!	Comments
Start Who Why What Future continuous How Jump start technique(s)					
Structure and organisation Clarity of timeline(s) Signposting					
Delivery					
Finish Signal Summary Conclusion Closing remarks Finish with a bang technique(s)					

Preparation and presentation

A   Read the brief and prepare your own presentation.

Full presentation practice: The chronological presentation

Subject and structure

Present a timeline describing past, present and future action.

Either:

- Present a work or personal (e.g. buying a new house, moving to another country) project.

    1   Give an overview of the project, outlining the background (the past).

    2   Then, move on to a comparison of the progress made up to now and the original plan and say what is happening now (the present).

    3   Finally, outline necessary future actions or strategies (the future).

Or:

- Present a system or process (e.g. the tax system in your country, the pensions system, health and safety procedures, a scientific, technical or manufacturing process).

    1   Say how the system or process operates now and outline its advantages and disadvantages (the present).

    2   Give the historical development of the system or process (the past).

    3   Give your proposal for the future operation of the system or process (the future).

Following a chronological order should dictate the structure of your presentation into a natural timeline. Use this structure as it's logical and simple.

Your audience

Choose your audience (e.g. your bosses, a parent company, an outside company, a subsidiary company, your local business club, undergraduate students). Before you start your presentation, tell the others in your group who your audience is.

Your targets

- To have a clear sense of purpose and to give all information in a clear structure
- To give accurate and informative timelines
- To have a good 'jump start' and 'finish with a bang'

B   Give your full presentation.

Feedback and targets

A   If you're working in a group, analyse each others' presentations, using the Feedback form below. If you're working alone, record yourself and analyse your own performance.

Feedback form: Connect with your audience					
	Poor	**OK**	**Good**	**Wow!**	**Comments**
Start					
Who					
Why					
What					
Future continuous					
How					
Jump start technique(s)					
Structure and organisation					
Clarity of timeline(s)					
Signposting					
Delivery					
Finish					
Signal					
Summary					
Conclusion					
Closing remarks					
Finish with a bang technique(s)					

Presentations diary

B   Look back at your feedback on your Step 2 presentation and, if possible, watch your presentation again. Now read 1–4 below and write your diary for Step 2.

1   What was positive for you? List three aspects and identify two new techniques you used successfully.

2   Identify one thing you could improve.

3   Identify one thing that didn't work for you.

4   Set yourself two targets for your next full presentation, including using one new technique from Step 2.

Step 3 Use visuals to connect

1 Visual aids

Introduction

A Here are four visual aids that Dan, Svitlana, Zhan and César used in their Step 3 presentations. Which worked most effectively do you think? Why?

1

2

3

4

B Which of these statements about PowerPoint slides do you agree with?

1   The presentation handout should not be the same document as the presentation slides.

2   It's OK if there are English spelling mistakes on a slide as no one expects me to be perfect.

3   You shouldn't use too many colours.

4   I need to include all details and data on my slides – that's my business and that's what my audiences expect!

5   A good presenter uses visual material to support the message and not to give the message.

6   I see and I remember.

7   The slides are the first thing I prepare as they're the most important part of my presentations.

8   If the slides are detailed enough, I can just read them aloud if I forget what I was going to say.

9   There should never be more than seven words on a slide.

10   The audience should listen to me and not worry about the slides too much.

11   A picture is worth a thousand words.

12   The audience can always read if they can't understand me.

13   Every visual aid should lead to my conclusion.

14   It's annoying and confusing if a presenter talks about subjects that are not even on the slide.

15   Less is more.

16   I appreciate it when the presenter doesn't rely on PowerPoint but does something a little different, such as using a flip chart or objects.

Find Your Voice

Write your own checklist for the use of visual information in presentations.

Interaction with visual aids

Number of slides

A 🔘 **3.01 Read the brief for the Step 3 presentation on page 47. Then watch Zhan's presentation and answer the questions.**

1 How many slides did Zhan use in his eleven-minute presentation?
2 Do you think there were too few, just enough or too many?
3 Can you identify any slides that could be removed?

Addressing the audience

B **Look at the photo of Zhan during his presentation.**

1 Do you think the audience were listening to Zhan or reading at this moment?
2 Did the slide help Zhan's English?
3 Did the slide help Zhan to present his information?
4 Does the slide <u>add</u> anything to the overall presentation and final conclusion?
5 Read the tip below. Did Zhan follow this advice?

Tip

TTT when you present visual information:
- Touch – indicate what is relevant on the slide
- Turn back to the audience, then …
- Talk to the audience and not to the screen or wall

C Look at the text in three of Zhan's slides below.

What is genetic data?

■ Our DNA consists of 4 bases A, C, T and G; so our genetic data is a string of these 4 letters, e.g. …AGGGGATTTAAA…

■ But at each genetic location a person can have 1 or 2 types, so can encode the genetic data in terms of 0 and 1s, e.g. …0101001010101…

Why do we simulate genetic data?

■ Lots of methods in literature about how to locate disease genes

■ To assess a method, apply it to data set and compare predicted location with actual location

■ But need data sets with known location of disease gene … not many of these

■ Use simulated data sets

Why is simulating genetic data challenging?

■ Real genetic data is not a random set of 0 and 1s

■ There are complex correlation structures due to thousands of years of evolution

■ Realistic simulated data should contain these structures

Grammatically inconsistent lists are confusing and difficult to follow. Simplify the text by (1) applying the 'less is more' principle and cutting the number of words and (2) making the bullet points grammatically consistent.

Examples

Bullet points starting with verbs	Bullet points starting with adjectives
• Attack market • Simplify product line • Cut prices	• Larger market • Simplified products • Reduced prices

Bullet points starting with nouns
• Market attack
• Simplification of product line
• Price reduction

Procedure

D 3.02 Zhan's presentation was a research report to statisticians who are experts on their subject, but have limited knowledge of biology. Watch Zhan's presentation of the three correlation matrices in his third point again. Do you like the way he presented these slides? Why / Why not?

E Zhan used a procedure to present each matrix. Identify the sequence by putting the following stages in the correct order 1–4.

He gives the message or conclusion. ....

He says what the most important part is. ....

He draws the audience's attention to the diagram. ....

He explains the matrix in general terms so that the audience can become familiar with it. ....

Now watch his presentation of the three matrices again and check your answers.

F What stages are these phrases from? Write the stage number from E next to the phrases.

1 I'd like us to focus our attention on … ....

2 What is interesting / important here is … ....

3 I'm sure the implications are clear to all of us … ....

4 The figures in this table show … ....

5 It is important to notice that … ....

6 The take-home message here is … ....

7 We can conclude that … ....

8 This chart compares … ....

9 I'd like you to think about … ....

10 If you look at the top right-hand corner … ....

11 The lesson we can learn from this is … ....

12 The blue dotted line represents … ....

13 The top half shows … ....

14 Now, I'll show you … ....

15 Let's move on now and look at the figures for … ....

16 The significance of this is … ....

17 I would like you to concentrate on this green column … ....

18 The next overhead shows … ....

19 As we can see … ....

20 The vertical axis represents … ....

Find Your Voice

Highlight the expressions that you would like to learn first and prepare three visual aids from a presentation that you could give in your work or study situation. Use the procedure above, making a clear transition from one slide to the next. When you are ready, present your visual information.

Take a risk!

G 🔘 3.03 **Watch Zhan's 'finish'. He had one slide projected during his summary and conclusion. Answer the questions.**

1 Did the summary chart make his summary clearer?

2 What was Zhan's conclusion?

3 Did the visual aid (summary chart) Zhan used add a 'bang' to his final message?

H 🔘 3.04 **Now, watch Svitlana's 'finish' to her Step 3 presentation. She briefed UK students on their upcoming trip to India. Answer the questions.**

1 What did Svitlana use as visual aids?

2 Compare her 'finish' to Zhan's. Do you think her message had more 'bang'?

Find Your Voice

Prepare a point in a presentation or take a point from your Step 2 presentation. Illustrate your point by using one or more unusual visual aids that can add power to your content. Take a risk! When you are fully prepared, stand up and present your point with the visual aid(s).

Assess your performance by answering these questions.

1 How did you feel?

2 Did your use of visual aids add punch to your content?

3 Could you take a risk like this in your business or academic life?

2 Numbers and trends

Numbers and approximations

A **Read aloud 1–5 and pronounce them clearly.**

1 4,579 employees   2 30.33 metres   3 $995   4 7.385%   5 €5.1 million

B **Now read aloud 1–5 below.**

1 around 4,500 employees

2 just over 30 metres

3 $1,000 more or less

4 approximately 7.4%

5 roughly €5 million

C **Read the examples of approximations below.**

Our agency has worked on 1,024 brands.

Our agency has worked on over / just over / more than 1,000 brands.

The number of brands is just above 1,000.

Our agency has worked on approximately / about / round about / roughly / more or less 1,000 brands.

Our agency has worked on 1,994 brands.

Our agency has worked on well over / well above 1,000 brands.

Our agency has worked on nearly / just under / almost 2,000 brands.

Now read the tip below and present sentences 1–10, using approximations.

1 We have 693 offices in 153 cities worldwide.

2 Our revenue was €333.33 billion last year.

3 There was a 5.67% increase in sales.

4 Ingredients: 82.7% water.

5 78.9% stated a strong preference for Product Y.

6 Europe: last twelve months, category spending is $12.9 million, down 0.2%.

7 Total forecast value: £2,697.

8 Australia: 193,399 professional engineers.

9 Fast process: 22–29 seconds.

10 We manufacture a total of 721 different products.

Tip

If you give numbers during your presentation, you don't always need to give exact figures.
An audience can be confused by too much complexity, and you can give exact figures in
a handout after the presentation if these are necessary. Lead your audience to your conclusion
by using approximations.

Trends

A Brainstorm all the words you already know to describe the following graphs.

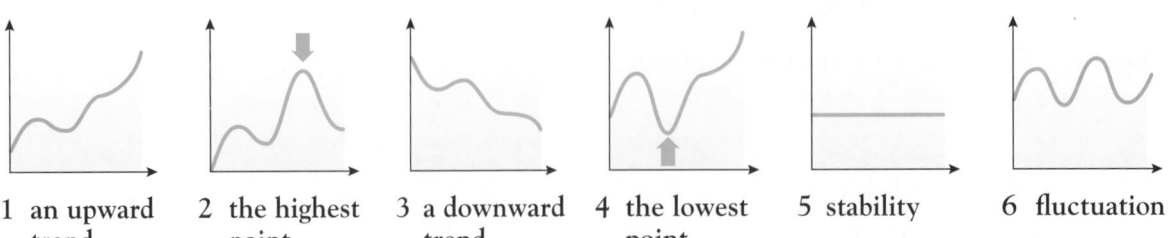

1 an upward trend 2 the highest point 3 a downward trend 4 the lowest point 5 stability 6 fluctuation

B Now look at page 110. Did you include all of these in your brainstorming? Add any new ones to your brainstorming lists in A.

C Complete the gaps in these presentation extracts, using vocabulary from B.

1 To our surprise, it was the sales of Product A that (1) t.......... .... over the Christmas period with sales 51% above target and Product B that (2) s.......... with sales 34% below target. As a result, we are redesigning the packaging for Product B and are forecasting that sales will (3) r.......... by Easter. If this does not happen and sales show no (4) i.........., we will seriously have to consider taking Product B off the market.

2 In this period, Brand A's market share (1) s.......... .... from 9% to 8% and Brand B's share (2) p.......... from 6% to just 1%. Our Brand Z (3) r.......... from 10% to 25%. If we look at the budget for TV advertising during this period, we can see clearly that Brand Z (4) d.......... its budget from €250,000 to €500,000. The print advertising budget (5) r.......... .... during the same period but was concentrated on the target market.

3 I'd now like to focus on the carbon dioxide content. Have a look at this graph. There have been (1) u.......... .... in the carbon dioxide content since the first unit was installed three years ago. It has (2) f.......... between 0.33% and 4% as we have experienced multiple failures. The units are now working efficiently and carbon dioxide content is (3) h.......... .... at 0.33% and we expect this to (4) s.......... at 0.2% by the end of the year.

4 Let's move onto the statistics. In 1900, 15% of the workforce was aged over 55 and by 2000 this had (1) g.......... .... to 33%. We expect this to (2) j.......... to roughly 40% by 2030. Life expectancy was approximately 46 years in 1900 but this has (3) s.......... .... to round about 80 today. What does this all mean for us when we look at the question of age diversity?

Tip

If you describe a lot of trends, use a wide variety of vocabulary and be dramatic. *Sales rocketed in the third quarter* is more dramatic and tells your audience more about the trend than *Sales increased in the third quarter*, for example.

Grammar

Adjectives and adverbs

A You can be even more dramatic by adding adjectives and adverbs to your trend descriptions. Brainstorm as many adjectives (*big, small, fast*) and adverbs (*well, badly, slowly*) as you can.

B Now look at page 111. Did you include all of these in your brainstorming? Add any new ones to your brainstorming lists in A.

C Choose the best adverb or adjective for each sentence.

1 Sales shot up *slowly / slightly / dramatically* and surpassed all our expectations.

2 The coverage rate decreased *significantly / slightly / steadily* by 10% every year.

3 There was a *huge / slight / significant* rise in unit price from €0.75 to €0.77.

4 The marketing department has grown *considerably / gradually / slowly* in the last three years and doubled its size.

5 A *fast / gradual / small* rise in raw material prices has slowly but surely eroded our margin.

6 Up to now we have ignored the *small / steady / rapid* growth in the sector but the growth is so fast that we cannot continue to do this.

7 There was a *sharp / gradual / fast* and noticeable jump in wastage in a very short time.

8 The online marketing costs are dropping *slightly / substantially / significantly*. However, the decline is so small that we shouldn't include it in the final figures.

Prepositions

D Complete this presentation extract with the correct prepositions.

Let's move on to the statistics. In the 1960s we spent about 25% of our household income on food, but this has now actually dropped (1) .... 10% (2) .... 15%. However, the proportion of the average food budget that we spend in restaurants and on takeaways has risen dramatically (3) .... 2% (4) .... 33% in the same period. Most importantly, I would like to point out that annual national expenditure on ready meals fluctuated somewhere (5) .... £250 million and £300 million just 10 years ago but this has now jumped (6) .... nearly £400 million (7) .... almost £700 million. This has resulted from an increase (8) .... 100% in the numbers of single households and a decline (9) .... the time we spend cooking our main meal. This was around 2.5 hours in the 60s but has fallen significantly and today stands (10) .... 15 minutes. What does all this mean for us in the packaging industry?

> ### Find Your Voice
>
> Prepare a graph or use a work presentation graph that has a lot of trend information. Present this, using a wide variety of vocabulary but also giving a clear message from the graph.

Describing timelines

Past simple

We use the past simple to talk about trends that happened in the past and that have now finished.
It is often used with words and phrases referring to finished periods of time (*last year, from 2003–2006, ten years ago, when we installed the new production process*).
Sales **fell** between 2000 and 2003.
Sales **increased** during the summer months last year.

Present perfect

We use the present perfect to talk about trends that started in the past and that haven't yet finished.
It is often used with words and phrases referring to unfinished periods of time (*since, for, this year*).
Sales **have risen** since 2003.
Sales **have deteriorated** this month.

Past perfect and past perfect continuous

We use the past perfect or past perfect continuous to talk about trends that had already happened before another event in the past.
Sales **had** already **improved** when we introduced the new product line in 2006.
Sales **had been fluctuating** before we streamlined the processes.

Present continuous

We use the present continuous to talk about trends and changes that are happening now or around now.
Sales **are improving** at the moment.
The sales figures **are getting** worse and worse.

will

We use *will* to predict future trends.
Sales **will** pick up next year.
Sales **won't** improve in some markets in the foreseeable future.

E   **Look at the graphs and complete these presentation extracts, using the correct form of the verbs in brackets.**

1 I'd like to show you the budget for sponsorship and event marketing in the last five years. As you can see, it was at about €1 million five years ago and (1) .... (climb) considerably in the next three years. But please note that it (2) .... (rocket) since then and is now at the €5 million mark. The budget (3) .... (go up) again next year.

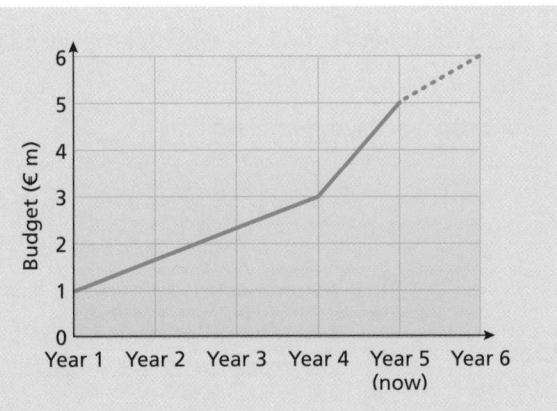

2 Let's take a detailed look at customer complaints about the hotline last year. We started with a total of 127 in January and this (1) .... (rise) sharply to 185 in April and this level (2) .... (remain) steady until June. The number (3) .... (reach) a peak in July with 250 during the summer holiday period. We introduced a three-shift system on the hotline at the end of December.

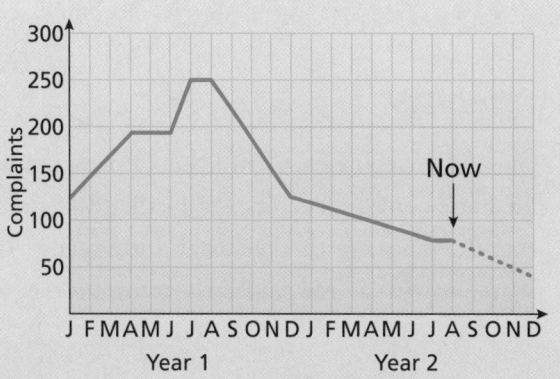

Complaints (4) .... (fall) dramatically before that but were still at an unsatisfactory level. I'm pleased to report that there (5) .... (be) a gradual drop in complaints since then. At the moment the number of complaints (6) .... (level off) a little but we believe that we (7) .... (hit) an all time low by December.

F Now, look at this graph and complete sentences 1–6, describing the sales. What tenses did you use and why?

1 .... last June.
2 .... before the joint venture.
3 .... last November.
4 .... from last November to now.
5 Now ....
6 .... next January.

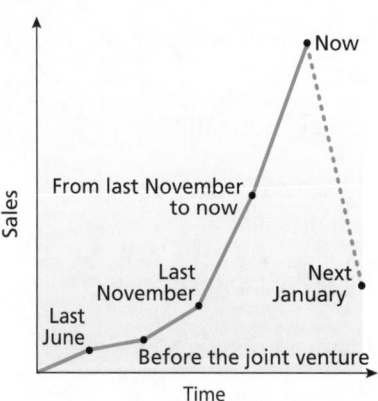

G Complete these forecasts for your organisation.

1 We expect …
2 I anticipate …
3 I forecast …
4 We foresee …
5 I predict …

Find Your Voice

Look at the brief for the full presentation for Step 3 on page 47. Prepare two charts that you could use for this brief, depicting change and a timeline. Present these:

• following the procedure you practised in E
• giving a clear message for both charts
• making a clear transition from one chart to the next
• using a good variety of vocabulary
• describing your timelines accurately and confidently

3 Full presentation

Analysis

A  3.05 Watch César's full Step 3 presentation to a business conference. The subject is trade dress. As you watch, rate the points in the Feedback form below. If you are working together with a group, discuss your analysis with the group.

Feedback form: Use visuals to connect					
	Poor	**OK**	**Good**	**Wow!**	**Comments**
Start Jump start technique(s)					
Structure and organisation Three-in-three structure					
Visual information Presentation of visual information Clarity of information Clarity of message					
Delivery Verbal garbage					
Finish Finish with a bang technique(s)					

Preparation and presentation

A   Read the brief and prepare your own presentation.

Full presentation practice: A review or report

Subject and structure

Either:

- Present a review (e.g. a product review, a review of an international law, a review of your industry, a media review, a review of local networking opportunities)

Or:

- Present a market report

Or:

- Present a research report

Feel free to use your imagination. However, you should be familiar with the topic area so that you can concentrate on the targets for this presentation.

Use this Three-in-three structure and make the structure clear for your audience.

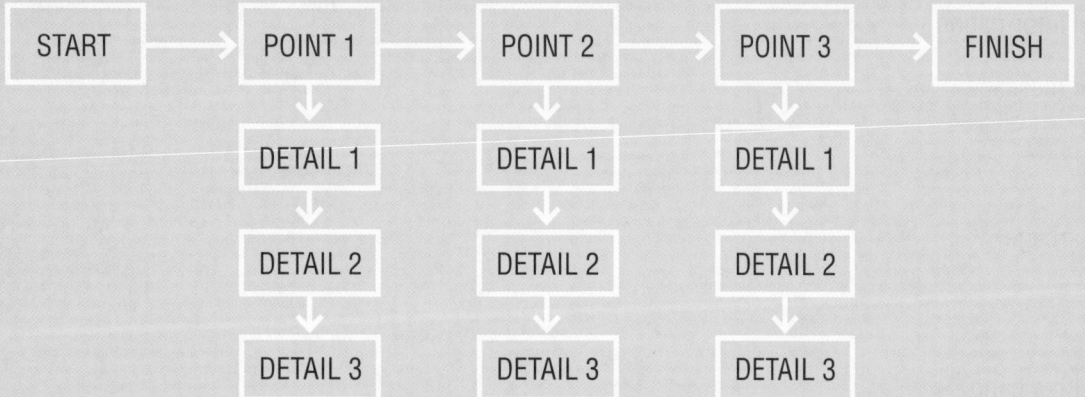

Prepare some visual information (pictures, charts, diagrams, objects) for your presentation. However, don't prepare an information overload and keep to an absolute maximum of nine charts – Keep It Short and Simple (KISS).

Your audience

Your audience is a very important (potential) client or group of (potential) clients. Before you start your presentation, tell the others exactly who your audience are.

Your targets

- To give all information in a clear structure
- To have a good 'jump start' and 'finish with a bang'
- To present effective visual information effectively

B   Give your full presentation.

Feedback and targets

A   If you're working in a group, analyse each others' presentations, using the Feedback form below. If you're working alone, record yourself and analyse your own performance.

Feedback form: Use visuals to connect					
	Poor	OK	Good	Wow!	Comments
Start Jump start technique(s)					
Structure and organisation Three-in-three structure					
Visual information Presentation of visual information Clarity of information Clarity of message					
Delivery Verbal garbage					
Finish Finish with a bang technique(s)					

Presentations diary

B   Now you've finished the basics! You can lay solid foundations, connect with your audience and use visuals to connect. Look back at your feedback on your Step 3 presentation and, if possible, watch your presentation again. Now read 1–3 below and write your diary for Step 3.

1   Do you present visual information effectively? List three positive points.

2   List two things that you have to revise or do some work on to improve your presentation of visual material.

3   Set yourself two targets for your next full presentation.

Step 4 Top up your techniques

1 Powerful techniques

Introduction

A Read this extract from a presentation. The presenter works in the human resources department of a multinational manufacturer. The audience are potential graduate recruits.

Summit Programme Presentation Transcript　　　　Thursday, June 28

So, what is our second graduate programme?

This is our high potential Summit Programme that will take the best among you to the top, the very top. This is a very exciting option for those of you who are truly looking for variety, opportunity and challenge. The programme enables you to take on three different assignments in three countries in three years and at the same time study for postgraduate management and language qualifications.

It's a challenge, a real challenge. Your first assignment takes place in your home country, the second at our headquarters in San Diego and the third in another country where we expect you to learn a new language. Of course, we pay for all your relocation and study expenses. In fact, our support is very generous, very generous, indeed more generous than anything else you'll find on the job market. But, in return you have to be flexible, hard-working and self-motivated because this programme is not a holiday but a boot camp. You will work, work, work and study, study, study. We test you and you test us. If you successfully finish the three assignments, you are not simply at the end of your training, but at the beginning of a fast, interesting and rewarding career path on your way to the top, the very top.

Let me give you an example of a Summit success story. This is Milena Gawczynski. She had the best degree of her year from Warsaw University and a MBA that she completed during her year with us in San Diego. Her third year on the Summit Programme was spent in Barcelona where she initiated a project to improve communications between our southern European manufacturing plants. She speaks fluent Polish, Russian, English and Spanish and is currently head of our Central European Services office in Prague.

As you can see, our standards are much higher than other companies. Our assessment centre is far more rigorous than all the others presented to you today. That's because we only want the best and of course you'll get the best from us. Our 'summiteers' earn above average salaries and performance bonuses. Our mentoring scheme, international networks and development programme are second to none. If it's variety, opportunity and challenge you're looking for and you know you are the best, then, our Summit Programme is the one for you. It's the only one that will take you to the top, the very top.

HR Department

B Now read the presentation extract aloud. Which sections are more effective in speaking than in writing?

C Read what six presenters said about some of their favourite techniques they learnt on a presentations seminar. Then answer the questions below.

1   When we're presenting, it can feel unnatural to say the same words over and over again. But, I've noticed that **repetition** really works when I listen to a presentation. It really helps to clarify and consolidate the key points. So, I try to use repetition myself. I think if you can get over the 'unnatural' feeling, it's a really easy technique and it actually makes presenting in English less difficult as you don't have to find different words for the same things.

2   You can repeat a phrase or a slogan like a **mantra**. Sometimes it's this mantra that everyone remembers long after the presentation is over. I learnt that classical orators used this technique and I think one of the most famous modern examples is the Martin Luther King speech where he used the 'I have a dream' mantra. People even call it the 'I have a dream' speech. Mantra has to be precise, to the point and memorable. When you get the mantra right, everyone remembers it.

3   I quite like using **rhetorical questions** as they create expectation and a feeling of dialogue. They're also a useful tool for outlining or signposting the structure. You should use grammatically correct questions though if you're presenting in another language. It's no good asking a question if the audience don't understand it or because you asked something too complex.

4   I really remember the **Rule of Three**. It's so easy. Good presentations often have lists with three different words, three identical words, three phrases or three sentences. Most experts attribute the Rule of Three to Aristotle's Art of Rhetoric in which he referred to 'three types of speeches' and 'three forms of proof'. Pythagoras said three was the 'perfect number'. Lists of three have a sense of completeness and research shows that listeners wait for and expect a third item in a list. As a presenter, I think it's a fairly simple but highly effective technique.

5   One of the things I like to do is give real life **examples** or examples that everybody knows. I think this really 'speaks' to the audience as they remember things when they relate them to themselves, events or people. Examples bring things to life. It's all about creating associations.

6   A number of effective techniques we use today go right back to the classical writers on rhetoric. Take **contrast**, for example – if you compare one thing to another, you are making a contrast. 'We are bigger than our competitors' is an example. Another contrast technique is to use words that are opposites. Kennedy did it in that famous speech, 'symbolizing an end not a beginning' and 'United, there is little we cannot do … Divided, there is little we can do'. He used 'not … but' in the same speech too, 'We observe today not a victory of party but a celebration of freedom'. From a language point of view, these are really not complicated techniques for non-native speakers to use.

1   Can you find examples of techniques 1–6 in the presentation transcript in A on page 50?
2   Do you already use any of techniques 1–6 in your presentations?
3   Which new techniques would you be able to incorporate in your presentations?
4   Would you find any of the techniques difficult to use?

Repetition, repetition

A The written statement below can be presented in a number of different ways depending on the point the presenter wants to stress.

We need a fundamental change in management strategy.

Now read these examples aloud and pause for two seconds before the repetition.

What we need, what we need is a fundamental change in management strategy.

We need a fundamental change in management strategy, in management strategy.

It's a fundamental, a fundamental change that we need in management strategy.

We need a fundamental change in management strategy, a fundamental change in management strategy.

B Read these points from Svitlana and César's Step 4 presentations.

Svitlana

1 You will drive back home or wherever you are going afterwards carefully, even if you are late.

2 Who makes it dangerous? You my dear people, car drivers, taxi drivers and bus drivers. You my dear people make life of cyclists every day's challenge.

3 Remember however in a hurry you are, your passengers are, there are definitely more important things to life than being on time.

4 Which means that you've got a much better chance to knock down a cyclist.

5 They don't give you the right of not being careful, to overtake cyclists sharply or to break speed limits even when the roads look empty.

6 Big bus, big danger.

César

1 Intellectual property is undeniably present in every single part of our lives.

2 Whatever we do, wherever we are, whatever we see or hear is all related to intellectual property.

3 The current situation really makes us wonder whether the countries which so ferociously promote intellectual property, and want to have their own creations protected, are consistent with the way intellectual property originated.

4 Back then intellectual property protection was non-existent compared to our 21st century, for example, where IP laws are literally omnipresent.

5 I cannot really see any reason why we should continue to perpetuate this by giving loads of protection to some and increasing the losses of other.

6 Intellectual property rights last a very long time.

7 The drive for monopoly is very strong.

4.01 Now watch Svitlana and César making the points above in extracts from their Step 4 presentations. Highlight the words or phrases they repeated in the presentations.

C 4.01 Watch the extracts again. Does repetition add clarity and impact to the statements?

> **Find Your Voice**
>
> Choose a topic from your Step 3 presentation and write three examples of repetition. Present them, using variation in stress and pace (speed). When you want to emphasise a point, use a slower pace.

Mantra

A 🔊 **4.02** **Svitlana compared three forms of transport in her Step 4 presentation. Can you suggest a mantra for this topic? Now watch the presentation extracts and answer the questions.**

1 What was Svitlana's mantra?

2 Is this mantra 'precise, to the point and memorable'?

3 Can you improve the mantra?

> **Find Your Voice**
>
> Develop a mantra for your Step 1, Step 2 and / or Step 3 presentations.

Rhetorical questions

A **Read the statements below and write a rhetorical question that could go <u>before</u> each of them.**
Example
We employ around 150 people in China.   *How many people do we employ?*

1 We employ around 150 people in China.

2 Last year we hired 50 new engineers in the Netherlands.

3 We are currently recruiting ten new sales office staff.

4 We are going to start recruiting for the Hong Kong office in June next year.

5 One solution is to use consultants to examine the problem.

6 No, we've never used an external company on this kind of project.

7 I strongly recommend buying a new office building.

8 The next step is to arrange a meeting with the client.

9 In my second point I'll be looking at where we can go from here.

10 I am now going to deal with this in my third point.

B **Read the statements below and write a rhetorical question that could go <u>after</u> each of them.**
Example
We've solved the problem.   *How did we do this?*

1 We've solved the problem.

2 The client insists that we increase internal security.

3 The plant has had its best year as regards safety.

4 We are going to have to go after new business in the next year.

5 That brings me to the end of my second point.

6 We have increased market share in Europe.

7 However, we have lost market share in North America.

8 This is the not the first time we have made such a mistake.

9 To tell the truth I found this quite a difficult task.

10 We thought it was the best campaign we had ever created but the client hated it!

C Correct the rhetorical questions.

1 What means this?
2 What did we have done?
3 How often speak you English in meetings?
4 Does the client accepts our changes?
5 Did we made the changes?
6 What does we doing about this?

Delivery: Intonation in questions

D 4.03 Watch an extract from César's Step 4 presentation. Note how he used a rising tone at the end of these rhetorical questions, adding impact to his message.

Is not a lifetime enough to recoup what you have invested in? ↗

Do we really need to give them another 100 years? ↗

Are we not actually going too far? ↗

> **Find Your Voice**
>
> Prepare one point from a presentation. Incorporate three rhetorical questions. Then present your point, using a rising tone at the end of the rhetorical questions.

Rule of Three

A Brainstorm lists of three that you know from literature, speeches, sayings, advertising slogans, etc.

B 4.04 Watch the following presentation extracts from Svitlana's Step 4 presentation and complete the lists of three that she uses.

1 Let's start then. Let's look at cycling first. Cycling is ....
2 You, you my dear people make life of cyclists every day's ...., every day's ...., every day's ....
3 You need to be even more careful. I ....
4 that you ...., a tight schedule, that your passengers ...., if you don't overtake a slow cyclist, that you are ...., of cyclists jumping the red light.
5 The only recommendation I can make and I insist on you following it is: ....

> **Find Your Voice**
>
> Write three examples for your Step 3 presentation. The last element in a list is often the most important one. Present these, stressing the last point in your list. Use pacing and pausing.

Examples

A 4.05 Watch an extract from César's Step 4 presentation and answer the questions.

1 Which example did César use?
2 Was the example relevant?
3 Did it add clarity to his point?

Contrast

Grammar: Comparisons

Form
One-syllable adjectives and some two-syllable adjectives have a comparative ending in *-er*. *China is a smaller market for us than India.*
Two-syllable adjectives ending in *-y* have a comparative ending in *-ier*. *It'll be easier to break into India than into China.*
Normally two-syllable adjectives use *more* in the comparative. *The plant in India is **more modern** than the one in China.*
Longer adjectives with more than three syllables always use *more* in the comparative. *On the whole India is **more interesting** than China.*
These are common irregular forms. good → better   bad → worse   far → further, farther

A Complete these comparisons with the correct form of the word in brackets.

1 Product Y is .... than Product X. (good)

2 Campaign 1 is .... than Campaign 2. (appealing)

3 The situation is .... than we anticipated. (bad)

4 The plant we have just bought is actually .... than the old one. (big)

B Write a word or phrase with the same meaning next to the words below.

just   a little   much   roughly

1 slightly ....

2 considerably ....

3 virtually ....

4 exactly ....

C Now complete the recommendations below with a word from exercise B.

Option A: 90€	Option B: 50€	Option C: 45€	Option D: €50

1 We recommend Option C as this is .... cheaper than Option A.

2 We recommend Option C as this .... cheaper than Option B.

3 We recommend Option C as this is .... half the price of Option A.

4 We recommend Options B and C, which are very similar. They're .... the same.

Find Your Voice

Read the brief for the Step 4 presentation on page 59. Write three comparisons for one of the Step 4 presentation subjects. Present them using stress and appropriate pace.

Opposites

D **Many parts of speech – not just adjectives – have opposites.**

*You should **always** prepare your presentations and **never** rely on PowerPoint. (adverb)*

*We need to **attack** the competition and not just **defend** our market position. (verb)*

*We don't want to be **behind** the curve, but **in front** of it. (preposition)*

*The change in the law was the reason for their **failure** and our **success**. (noun)*

Write the opposites of these words.

1	dark	5	before	9	start	13	day	17	old
2	strong	6	truth	10	up	14	good	18	love
3	right	7	live	11	tall	15	success	19	early
4	fast	8	hot	12	give	16	forbid	20	top

Find Your Voice

Write three statements including dramatic use of opposites from the list above for one of the Step 4 presentation subjects. Present them, stressing the words that are opposites and using appropriate pace.

Not X but Y

E **Look at this example.**

*The changes we have made are designed **not** to confuse **but** to simplify.*

🔘 **4.06 Now watch Svitlana present three points from the Step 4 presentation.**

1 I don't argue the fact that you might have a very good reason to pollute … but when your kids grow up, …

2 You have to not only obey the road rules, but take care of the people on the road.

3 Because you are responsible not only for your life, but for the lives of your passengers as well.

Delivery: Pace

F **Read Svitlana's statements aloud stressing the words *not* and *but*. Use a slower pace pausing at //.**

1 I don't argue // that you might have // a very good reason to pollute // but when your kids grow up, …

2 You have to // not only obey the road rules // but take care of // the people on the road.

3 Because you are responsible // not only for your life // but for the lives of your passengers as well.

Find Your Voice

Write three *not … but* contrasts for one of the Step 4 presentation subjects. Try to make them short and to the point. Present them, using stress and an appropriate pace.

Advanced signposting

A Match the signposts with the examples.

1 change direction and / or depart from the original plan of your presentation

2 refer to an earlier point

3 refer to a point that is coming later

4 repeat something

5 give a wider perspective

6 give a deeper analysis

7 give just the basic information

a I'd like to expand / elaborate on that …

b Let's just recap …

c Let me digress for a moment …

d Let me put that in a nutshell …

e I'd like to go back to a point I mentioned earlier …

f I'll be coming to that later …

g Let me give you another example …

Find Your Voice

The written statements below are taken from an Annual Report. Work with a partner and make the statements more interesting and dramatic for a spoken presentation. Incorporate techniques from Step 4, changing the written style to a speaking style. Have fun with the exercise. Present the report together. If you are working with a group, assess which team gives the best presentation.

The Global Group took another major step forward last year. As a specialist in telecommunications we have moved into a new league with sales up by 23 per cent to €2.135 billion.

We have continued to strengthen our leading market positions all over the world. This positive progress is due to a number of reasons. Global has:

> made further inroads into the markets of Asia, Latin America and the Middle East

> successfully integrated newly acquired businesses into our own operations, with positive synergetic effects

> taken further action to restructure operations and cut costs

> initiated efficiency drives in the mobile phone products sector

> improved teamwork within the Global Group and with customers and suppliers under the 'Year of Sales' initiative, and increased our capacity for innovation.

Increasingly, our employees operate internationally and in international teams. Last year, we were faced with the particular challenge of integrating various newly acquired companies with the Global Group and of creating new organisational units. In the 'Year of Sales', we formed a number of additional interdisciplinary and cross-border project teams. For example, the Mobile Phone products business sector launched its 'Global Management Associates' project in which teams with employees from different countries jointly analyse work processes and develop best practice guidelines.

We are continuing to concentrate on superior products and solutions which set us apart from the rest of the competition. Our efforts remain geared towards strengthening our market potential through innovation, increasing our attractiveness to end consumers and trade alike, and identifying opportunities for expansion. We are well equipped to achieve sustained growth in both sales and earnings. Our objective for next year is to pass the €5 billion mark in sales revenue.

2 Full presentation

Analysis

A   🔘 4.07   Watch César's full Step 4 general public presentation on the subject of intellectual property. As you watch, rate the points in the Feedback form below. If you are working together with a group, discuss your analysis with the group.

Feedback form: Top up your techniques					
	Poor	OK	Good	Wow!	Comments
Start Jump start					
Structure and organisation Basic signpost language					
Finish Finish with a bang technique(s)					
Delivery Stress Pace Intonation					

B   Which of the following techniques did César use?

Technique	Yes / No	Detail
Repetition	Yes / No	....
Mantra	Yes / No	....
Rhetorical questions	Yes / No	....
Rule of Three	Yes / No	....
Examples	Yes / No	....
Contrasts	Yes / No	....

Preparation and presentation

A   Read the brief and prepare your own presentation.

Full presentation practice: Comparing information

Subject and structure

Choose one of the following or think of your own subject.

- three different forms of transport
- three different jobs or careers
- three different products
- three different advertising campaigns
- three technologies
- your country and two other countries
- your company and two other companies
- your university and two others

Compare the three items and make a recommendation.

Your structure should always be simple, logical and clear in order to navigate your audience to your conclusion. You have already used variations of the three-part structure which meet these basic criteria:

The three-part structure (Step 1)

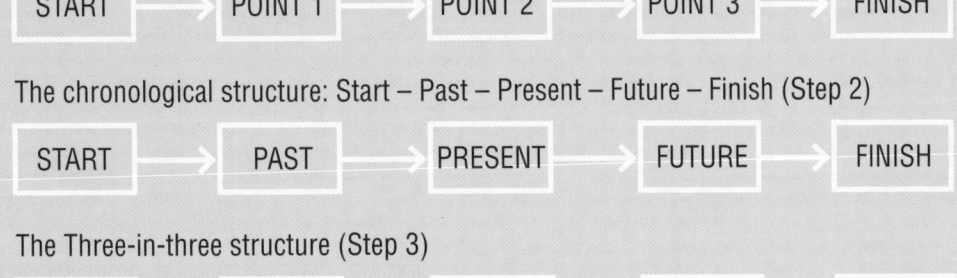

The chronological structure: Start – Past – Present – Future – Finish (Step 2)

The Three-in-three structure (Step 3)

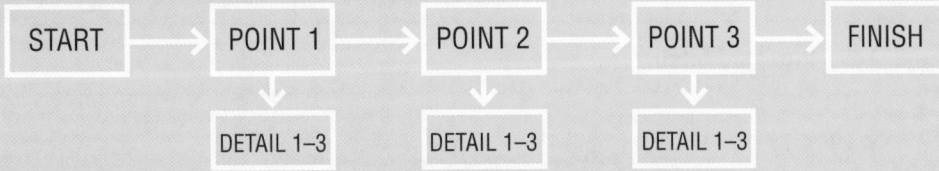

Think carefully how you are going to develop your information in a three-part structure in this presentation and how you are going to highlight the items or features you are comparing. Also, consider how you will draw attention to the positive factors and downplay negative factors when it comes to building your recommendation into the structure.

Your audience

Your audience comprise a very difficult group of people. You need to 'sell' your recommendation, using a variety of techniques.

Your targets

- To 'sell' your recommendation using rhetorical techniques effectively
- To have a clear logical structure that is clearly signposted and uses advanced signposting

B   Give your full presentation.

Feedback and targets

A If you're working in a group, analyse each others' presentations, using the Feedback form below. If you're working alone, record yourself and analyse your own performance.

Feedback form: Top up your techniques					
	Poor	OK	Good	Wow!	Comments
Start Jump start					
Structure and organisation Basic signpost language					
Finish Finish with a bang technique(s)					
Delivery Stress Pace Intonation					

Technique	Yes / No	Detail
Repetition	Yes / No	....
Mantra	Yes / No	....
Rhetorical questions	Yes / No	....
Rule of Three	Yes / No	....
Examples	Yes / No	....
Contrasts	Yes / No	....

Presentations diary

B Look back at your feedback on your Step 4 presentation and, if possible, watch your presentation again. Now read 1–3 below and write your diary for Step 4.

1 Did you use the new techniques effectively? List three positive points.

2 List two things you have to revise or work on to improve your presentation of visual material.

3 Set yourself two targets for your next full presentation.

Step 5 Be positive and dramatic

1 Be positive

Power words

The Yale 12

A A Yale University study identified the following words as the twelve most powerful words in the English language. Why do you think these words are powerful?

The Yale 12	
discover(y)	easy
guarantee(d)	health
love	money
new	proven
results	safety
save	you

B Put the words from the Yale 12 list into the gaps in the presentation extract below.

(1) .... are going to (2) .... the (3) .... features we have incorporated into our updated software package. As you will (4) .... , the software is very (5) .... to use and (6) .... from extensive testing have (7) .... its success. Its enhanced parental controls offer increased online (8) .... for children and also monitor the length of time spent online. You can compare these times with the World (9) .... Organisation's (WHO) maximum recommended times. In fact, we're so confident that we (10) .... that our software will (11) .... you both time and (12) ....

Common power words

C Brainstorm more power words. Check in the answer key on page 116 and see how many words you have included from the list of common power words.

Find Your Voice

Prepare to describe the features and benefits of a product or service, using as many of the Yale 12 and the other power words as possible. Present this.

Grammar

Conditional sentences

A   Read this presentation summary and answer the questions below.

So, we're now at the end of our presentation. Let's recap on the three options:

We've looked at the possibility of not moving offices at all and staying here in the middle of the city. There would be some minor benefits here as we would save money, but this would be for a limited time only. We have to look at the long term. Our company is expanding rapidly. We would lose credibility and market share if we decided to stay here.

Next, we looked at moving outside the city or even of moving to another country. Again, we've seen some advantages as this is an expensive city and we could find a cheaper location. However, our company has been in this city for a very long time and our whole identity is tied in with this location. If we moved to another location, our corporate identity would suffer greatly.

The third option is to stay in the city but to move to a state-of-the art building near the airport. If we build our own offices, we will strengthen our image, improve internal communications and provide room for further expansion and success whilst maintaining our basic structure and values.

1   Highlight the 'if' sentences the presenter uses.

2   Read the notes about conditionals below. Why does the presenter use both types in the presentation?

1st Conditional	2nd Conditional
If + present, will + infinitive	*If + past simple, would + infinitive*
We use the 1st conditional to talk about events and situations which might happen. *If we **get** the approval, we**'ll start** the process next week.*	We use the 2nd conditional to talk about events and situations which are unreal or unlikely to happen. *If the company **moved** to Shanghai, I **would get** another job.*

B   Complete these recommendations and proposals with your own ideas.

1   If we decided to go in this direction, …

2   If we wanted to do this, …

3   If we take this option, …

4   If you made a decision to go with XYZ, …

5   If you buy this product, …

6   If you continued in this way, …

7   If you employed an external company, …

8   If you simply restructure, …

Find Your Voice

Prepare and present three 'if' recommendations for a Step 5 presentation subject on page 73.

Convincing language

A Read the two proposals below. Highlight the words and phrases that make Proposal A tentative and Proposal B more positive and convincing.

Proposal A

Let me then turn to the third and final option which is to move to new offices near the airport. There are some drawbacks to this option as the process of finding a location, building to our specifications and moving will be costly and time-consuming. We shouldn't worry too much about these drawbacks though as the advantages outweigh the disadvantages. I suggest that we find a location where we can build to our specifications in a way that reflects our corporate image. Clients could get to our offices more easily from the airport and we should be able to build an underground garage so that there'll be more visitor parking. In addition, you find good accommodation around the airport. Hopefully, we could restructure the offices so that we maybe can improve internal communication and leave room for new departments as we perhaps grow. We should stick to our corporate values and many of our staff will probably stay with us.

Proposal B

Let me then turn to the third, final and best option which is to move to new offices near the airport. There could be some minor drawbacks to this option as the process of finding a location, building to our specifications and moving might be costly and time-consuming. We should not worry about these drawbacks though as the advantages far outweigh the disadvantages. I strongly recommend that we find a location where we can build to our specifications in a way that reflects our corporate image. Clients will get to our offices more easily from the airport and we are going to build an underground garage so that there will be more visitor parking. In addition, you do find good accommodation around the airport. What we'll do is restructure the offices so that we'll certainly improve internal communication and leave room for new departments as we grow. We plan to stick to our corporate values and to keep most of our staff.

B Make the statements below more convincing by changing or adding vocabulary.

1 I hope you understood my message.
2 Perhaps it will be successful.
3 We could do that for you.
4 This is an interesting idea.
5 Maybe we should go in that direction.
6 I think you should go with this campaign.
7 These findings might indicate we should do this.
8 You never know but it could be right.

C To strengthen your proposal, you can emphasise words that are often contracted and / or add and stress auxiliary verbs (*do, does, did*). Read this extract aloud stressing the words in bold.

We should **not** worry about these drawbacks though as the advantages far outweigh the disadvantages. Clients **will** get to our offices more easily from the airport and we are going to build an underground garage so that there **will** be more visitor parking. In addition, you **do** find good accommodation around the airport.

D Strengthen the statements by giving the full form of contracted words and / or adding auxiliaries.
1 I think it's time for a change.
2 We don't believe this is a good idea.
3 The candidate didn't meet our requirements.
4 He met all our requirements.
5 She's going to write a new specification.
6 This isn't an option I recommend.
7 The research shows that we have to modify the product.
8 What they're proposing isn't feasible.

Delivery

Pronunciation

A 🔘 5.01 You should always check the pronunciation of key words. Watch the first part of Svitlana's Step 5 presentation. Which key words does she pronounce incorrectly?

B 🔘 5.01 Read the transcript below for this extract. Watch the extract again and think about how to improve the stress, pronunciation problems and pacing.

So, let's start then. I will start by telling you what the greenhouse effect is. So, the greenhouse effect is the process by which absorption and emission of infra-red radiation by atmospheric gases warms a planet's atmosphere and surface. Sounds hot, doesn't it? On Earth the major natural greenhouse gases are water vapour which causes about 36–70% of greenhouse effects, it's also carbon dioxide 9–26% of greenhouse effects, methane 4–9% greenhouse effects and ozone 3–7% of greenhouse effect. The atmospheric concentration of carbon dioxide and methane have increased by 31 and 149% respectively above pre-industrial levels since 1715. This is considerably higher than at any time during the last 650,000 years, the period for which reliable data has been extracted from ice cores. Pretty scary picture, isn't it? And we need and can change it. How do we do that?

C Make the extract more convincing. Then, read your version aloud using the correct pronunciation.

> **Find Your Voice**
>
> Prepare and present a convincing proposal for a Step 5 presentation subject on page 73.

2 Be dramatic

Introduction

A Read the text below and answer the questions on page 67.

DRAMATIC PRESENTATIONS

 An expert presenter employs a whole range of additional techniques to help communicate the message.

What characterises an effective presenter?
Effective presenters do a competent job and give well-organised and well-structured presentations. They give solid information to their audiences and explain complex information effectively and logically. An expert presenter employs a whole range of additional techniques to help communicate the message.

Why do effective presenters need to learn more skills?
These presenters often put on their 'business face'. They tend to be formal and objective and this sometimes makes it difficult for audiences to follow and take in information. Such presenters can fail to truly inspire, connect and take their audiences to a different level.

What techniques can they use to inspire and connect?
They can incorporate imagery and storytelling and build on effective presentations by making memorable and striking similes, metaphors and analogy and by relating stories and anecdotes. This means they should give themselves enough time for preparation, be willing to drop the 'business face' and be creative, human and authentic.

If we look at imagery first, what's the difference between simile, metaphor and analogy?
A simile is a comparison between two things, using the word *like*, e.g. *The product is like a shooting star.*
A metaphor also makes a comparison, but doesn't use *like*, e.g. *The product is a shooting star.*
An analogy can be defined as an extended metaphor, e.g. *The product is a shooting star and is the brightest thing in the sky.*

How does imagery work?

The presenter takes two seemingly unrelated items and makes a comparison between them. There is a kind of shock effect and the audience begins to resolve this by making a connection between the two items. This creates pictures and associations, fires the imagination and brings the presentation to life. It's no surprise that imagery is often remembered long after a presentation is over.

What kind of presentations work well with imagery?

Imagery can be particularly useful for those presenters who have to make technical or specialised presentations; an effective simile or metaphor can help an audience to understand complex issues without using complex language.

What's a story?

It's a narrative with a beginning, middle and end that frequently brings up unanswered questions, crises or conflicts that are resolved by the end of the story. Humour can be a part of the narrative.

> " Stories are very powerful in organising and giving information and in creating meaning. "

Why do stories help audiences understand and remember information?

Stories are very powerful in organising and giving information and in creating meaning. It is easier to understand and recall information when it is part of the flow of a story and connected to other events in a narrative. A story builds a relationship between the audience and presenter and keeps the listeners engaged as they participate in the narrative, wanting to know what happens next and how the story ends. Emotions are addressed and this is also important for memory and learning since the emotional centre of the brain is situated near to the part of the brain responsible for long-term memory. In addition, stories put people in a state of relaxed awareness – an alpha state – which is a more receptive state for absorbing information. It's no coincidence that storytelling has a long oral tradition in most cultures!

What characterises a good storyteller?

Good storytellers are positive, enthusiastic and relate stories that make a relevant point. They make the message clear and make a connection between the story and the presentation.

What's an anecdote?

An anecdote can be defined as a true or a personal story that can also include self-disclosure. When a presenter discloses personal information, he / she shows a human side and the audience empathises. Anecdotes should not be too long or include too much detail. Ronald Reagan was known as 'The Great Communicator' and he used anecdotes extensively.

1   Do you already use imagery and storytelling techniques?

2   Do you think you put on a 'business face' when you present?

3   In principle, do you agree that imagery and storytelling should be used in presentations?

4   If you don't use imagery or storytelling, can you remember a presentation where a presenter used such techniques?

Techniques

Simile

A **Complete the similes.**

Example

A presentation is like a gift because *you need to think about the recipient and packaging the content.*

   1   A presentation is like a gift because …
   2   A presentation is like a road because …
   3   A presentation is like a forest because …
   4   A presentation is like a fairy story because …
   5   A presentation is like chewing gum because …
   6   A presentation is like an oyster because …
   7   Working in our industry is like playing football because …
   8   Our organisation is like a ship because …
   9   My job is like a banana because …
  10   My team is like …
  11   Our main competitor is like …
  12   Our main product is like …

Metaphor and analogy

B 🔘 **5.02 Watch an extract from Zhan's Step 5 presentation. Zhan presented his research to an audience of non-specialists.**

   1   Describe Zhan's metaphor / analogy in your own words.
   2   Was his analogy clear and simple?
   3   Did the analogy get your attention?

C **Develop and extend the metaphors below.**

   1   two methods as apples and oranges
   2   a process as a journey
   3   a job as a book
   4   customer service as a game of golf
   5   the problem as mice, the solution as a cat, a competitor's solution as a dog

---

Find Your Voice

Find a metaphor / analogy to describe an aspect of your work or area of study to a group of non-specialists. Develop this. Take your time – Zhan developed his analogy over some days. Present this.

Tell me a fact and I'll learn. Tell me the truth and I'll believe.
But tell me a story and it will live in my heart forever.
Indian Proverb

D   Read this story and check the meaning and pronunciation of any words you don't know or don't know how to pronounce.

CIRCUS ELEPHANTS

I recently went to the circus and after the show wandered around the animal enclosures. There were two fully grown elephants tethered to stakes in the ground in one enclosure. However, these elephants were not held with big heavy chains as you would expect but with quite small ones. It seemed to me that these huge elephants could easily walk away from their chains without much effort or without even breaking into a sweat. But surprisingly, the big, old elephants made no attempt to break away or to leave the enclosure.

In the next enclosure there was a tiny baby elephant tethered with exactly the same size of chain. This was quite a big chain for the baby elephant but it was doing its best to break away. It was pulling and pulling, making a lot of noise and doing absolutely everything it could to be free.

The animal trainer came by. He explained that the older elephants had given up trying to be free by breaking the chains. They had learnt that there was no point in fighting a long time ago and now believed they couldn't break the chains. The baby elephant was still motivated to break the chain and believed it could be free one day.

E   Retell the story in your own words.

F   The story is about fixed patterns of behaviour, being tied to the past and doing what you have always done. The baby elephant wants to initiate change and is motivated to do this.
Could you use this story to illustrate a presentation for your organisation?

G   🔘 5.03 Watch an extract from Svitlana's Step 5 presentation about greenhouse gases.
Answer the questions below.

1   Did Svitlana tell the story well? Why? / Why not?
2   Did she pronounce any words incorrectly?
3   How did she link the story to her presentation on page 65?
4   Was this link effective?

H Read these three stories. Then, complete the *Find Your Voice* exercise below.

Music History

Decca Records auditioned two groups at their London studios on New Year's Day in 1962. After the audition Decca decided to take on the local band, The Tremeloes. Dick Rowe, head of Decca's pop division, rejected the second group saying, 'We don't like their sound and guitar music is on the way out'. This second group was a Liverpool band called The Beatles. They went on to sign with Parlophone Records and from there to become the biggest success in pop history. Dick Rowe went down in music history as the man who rejected The Beatles.

The Fox and The Grapes

One hot summer's day a fox was strolling through an orchard when he came to a bunch of grapes just ripening on a vine on a very high branch. 'That's just what I need for my thirst,' the fox thought. Going back a few steps, he took a run and a jump, and just missed the grapes. Turning round again, he jumped up with a 'one, two, three', but with no success. He tried to get the grapes again and again but in the end gave up. The fox walked away with his nose in the air, saying, 'I am sure they're sour.'

Failure produces Success

One summer holiday my parents decided to send me for swimming lessons. It didn't take long to discover that I was a natural. I absolutely loved the water, was able to swim during my first lesson and swam 25 metres by the third lesson. The teacher recommended me for membership of a swimming club. I looked forward to every training session and soon was the fastest swimmer in my age group at the club.

The next step was to put me forward for the national championships. I trained and trained and trained. Everyone around me was really confident that I would win the championship or at the very least win a medal. At the championships I won my heats easily and found myself in the line-up for the final. It was really exciting to be standing in front of a large crowd and I felt very proud and happy as I soaked in the atmosphere – the cheers as the finalists were announced, the colours of the flags from different clubs and my parents and brothers waving to me from the stands. Then, the starter signalled the start of the race. Somehow, I must have got distracted and I missed diving in at the signal. In fact, I was the last swimmer to enter the water. I never caught up and finished last.

Looking over at the jubilant winner, I just couldn't believe it. I had failed and moreover, had failed really badly. As I could hardly drag myself out the water, my coach came over to help me. I muttered something about him dropping me from the team. I never forgot what he said next, 'Why would I drop you from the team? You're a great swimmer and you've learnt a huge lesson in just a few minutes. Winning is all about total focus and you'll never lose focus again.'

He was completely right. It was one of the best things that ever happened to me. I never lost focus again. That spectacular failure taught me all I needed to know in order to succeed and I went on to become a very successful national swimmer.

Find Your Voice

- Choose a subject from the brief for the Step 5 presentation on page 73 and a story above.
- Check pronunciation and practise telling the story in your own words.
- Link the story to your presentation.
- Present the story and the link.

Anecdote

I **5.04 Watch an extract from Zhan's Step 5 presentation and answer 1–4 below.**

1 Describe the two newspaper articles in your own words.

2 How did the articles link to his presentation?

3 Do you find the anecdotes engaging and relevant to the presentation?

4 Is there anything you would change?

Find Your Voice

Get some newspapers, magazines and newsletters. Find an interesting article that is relevant to one of the Step 5 presentation subjects on page 73. Relate the anecdote in your own words and link it to the Step 5 presentation. Present this.

Self disclosure

J **Read the story *Failure produces Success* on page 70 again. Answer the questions below.**

1 What do you learn about the presenter?

2 Do the personal anecdotes make her more human and do you empathise with her?

3 What message does she give with this anecdote?

Find Your Voice

'Just a Minute'

- Relate a personal anecdote about something funny, dangerous or interesting that happened to you and / or says something about you.

- Your targets are to limit the anecdote to one minute, to speak fluently and to eliminate verbal garbage.

- Record yourself and assess your performance or get feedback from colleagues.

- Do the task again if you don't manage to meet the targets.

K **5.05 Read the brief for the Step 1 presentation on page 21 again and read the brief for the Step 5 presentation on page 73. Then watch Zhan's complete Step 1 and Step 5 presentations and answer the questions below.**

1 Which style of presentation do you personally prefer?

2 Why do you prefer this presentation?

3 Are there any techniques that Zhan used or anything that he did that you could comfortably include in your own presentations?

4 Is there anything you can experiment with yourself?

3 Full presentation

Analysis

A 🔘 5.06 Watch Dan's full Step 5 presentation. His audience were a small group at a seminar and his subject is environmental issues. As you watch, rate the points in the Feedback form below. If you are working together with a group, discuss your analysis with the group.

Feedback form: Be positive and dramatic					
	Poor	**OK**	**Good**	**Wow!**	**Comments**
Start					
Structure and organisation					
Visual information					
Rhetorical techniques					
Finish					

B Watch again. Which of the following techniques did Dan use?

Technique	Yes / No	Detail	Technique	Yes / No	Detail
Yale 12	Yes / No		Metaphor and analogy	Yes / No	
Common power words	Yes / No		Storytelling	Yes / No	
Convincing language	Yes / No		Anecdote	Yes / No	
Simile	Yes / No		Self disclosure	Yes / No	

C 🔘 5.07 Dan and Svitlana independently chose to present environmental issues in their Step 5 presentations. Watch Svitlana's Step 5 presentation and answer the questions below.

1 Who gave a better presentation in your opinion? Why?

2 Who gave the clearer message? Why?

3 Who has the better relationship with the audience in your opinion? Why?

4 What are the advantages and disadvantages of working with a script?

Preparation and presentation

A   Read the brief and prepare your own presentation.

Full presentation practice: A proposal for change

Subject and structure

Choose one of the following or develop your own topic related to your particular field of work.

- retirement
- globalisation
- training in my company
- a product design and / or packaging and / or branding
- education in my country
- a company's corporate identity
- office allocation and design
- funding
- research
- part-time and temporary work – portfolio careers

Use this framework:

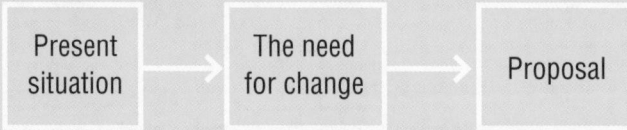

and one of the structures from steps 1–3.

Your audience

Either:

You've made arrangements to give this presentation to members of your organisation since you feel strongly about your proposal.

Or:

Your boss or professor has arranged for you to give this presentation at an external industry conference.

Your targets

- To have a good 'jump start'
- To have a clear structure and balanced arguments building to a convincing proposal
- To be positive and dramatic
- To use other techniques where necessary
- To 'finish with a bang'
- To persuade your audience that you have the right vision

B   Give your full presentation.

Feedback and targets

A   If you're working in a group, analyse each others' presentations, using the Feedback form below. If you're working alone, record yourself and analyse your own performance.

Feedback form: Be positive and dramatic					
	Poor	**OK**	**Good**	**Wow!**	**Comments**
Start					
Structure and organisation					
Visual information					
Rhetorical techniques					
Finish					

Technique	Yes / No	Detail	Technique	Yes / No	Detail
Yale 12	Yes / No		Metaphor and analogy	Yes / No	
Common power words	Yes / No		Storytelling	Yes / No	
Convincing language	Yes / No		Anecdote	Yes / No	
Simile	Yes / No		Self disclosure	Yes / No	

Presentations diary

B   Look back at your feedback on your Step 5 presentation and, if possible, watch your presentation again. Now read 1–4 below and write your diary for Step 5.

1   Did you persuade your audience? List three positive points.

2   Did you put on a 'business face'? Were you creative, human and authentic?

3   List two things that you can do to be more convincing.

4   Set yourself two targets for your next full presentation.

Step 6 Love your audience ... not everyone is like you

1 Something for everyone

Left and right brain

A   Brain research reveals that both sides of the brain are involved in nearly every human activity, but that the left and right sides of the brain control different modes of thinking. Look at statements 1–8 below and circle the letter of the statement that is true for you.

1   A I am objective.   B I am subjective.
2   A I like to take risks.   B I don't like to take risks.
3   A I am analytical.   B I am emotional.
4   A I am organised.   B I tend to break the rules.
5   A I like to use numbers.   B I like to use metaphors.
6   A I like to stick to the plan.   B I like surprises.
7   A I need the small details.   B I need the big picture.
8   A I am realistic.   B I am imaginative.

Now look at the information on page 122. Are you more 'left brained' or 'right brained'?

B   Look at the following activities from this book. Assign the activities to the left (L) or right (R) brain.
Step 1: giving your presentation a structure and using signposting ....
Step 2: jump starting your presentation with a shocking statement ....
Step 3: describing trends and numbers accurately and in detail ....
Step 4: using examples ....
Step 5: using analogy ....

C   Look at the table below. Tick what you do in your presentations. Is one side more dominant?

Left brain	Right brain
1 I give logical and precise information.	1 I include surprises and an element of play. ....
2 I give my research references.	2 I show lots of pictures. ....
3 I give lots of numbers and data.	3 I include metaphors and analogy. ....
4 I demonstrate that I am an expert.	4 I include lots of variety. ....
5 I have a very organised approach.	5 I move along at a fast pace. ....
6 I keep to time limits and scheduling.	6 I like to give the bigger picture. ....
7 I stay on track.	7 I deal with concepts. ....
8 My presentations are well-structured.	8 I address emotions and feelings. ....
9 I give lots of examples.	9 I move around a lot. ....
10 I let audiences evaluate and assess.	10 I let audiences experiment. ....

Find Your Voice

List five techniques / activities you can build into your presentations to create a better balance.

Representational systems

A   Read the text and then complete the exercise below.

VAKOG

We re-experience or represent the world to ourselves using our senses:

Visual	(V)	seeing
Auditory	(A)	hearing
Kinaesthetic	(K)	feeling
Olfactory	(O)	smelling
Gustatory	(G)	tasting

When we use our senses inwardly to think, they're known as representational systems in NLP (Neuro Linguistic Programming) …

The **visual** system is how we create our internal pictures, visualise, daydream, fantasise and imagine. When you are imagining looking around one of your favourite places or remembering being on the white sandy beach on holiday, or planning how your room will look, you are using your visual system.

The **auditory** system is how you remember music, talk to yourself and rehear the voices of other people. Auditory thinking is often a mixture of words and other sounds. When you imagine the voice of a friend, the roar of the sea or the sound of silence, you are using your auditory system.

The **kinaesthetic** system is made up of our internal and external feelings of touch and bodily awareness. It also includes the sense of balance. The emotions are also part of the kinaesthetic system, although emotions are slightly different – they're feelings about something, although they're still represented kinaesthetically in the body. When you imagine balancing on a beam, the feeling of touching a smooth surface or what it is like to feel completely happy, you are using your kinaesthetic system. Sometimes the olfactory and gustatory systems are treated as part of the kinaesthetic system, as they're less important in western Europe and North American culture.

The **olfactory** system deals with creating smells and the **gustatory** system is made up of remembered and created tastes. Remember a fine meal. Think back to what it was like to smell and taste the food. You are using your olfactory and gustatory systems.

Most people have a preferred representational system. We think more easily and more fluently with our preferred system.

Categorise the words and phrases below and on page 78. Do they appeal to visual (V), auditory (A), kinaesthetic (K), olfactory (O) or gustatory (G) representational systems?

1 It looks like … ………
2 It feels like … ………
3 Picture this … ………
4 It tastes like … ………

5 It smells like … ………
6 Can you hear this in your mind? ………
7 Imagine … ………
8 Think of the smell of … ………

9   What does this look like? ....

10   Think of the feeling when … ....

11   The aroma … ....

12   My perspective … ....

13   Think of the sound of … ....

14   What is it like to taste? ....

15   Do you feel happy / sad / disappointed? ....

16   How loud is it? ....

17   It's as high as a two-storey building. ....

18   The fragrance … ....

19   What do you say to yourself when things go wrong? ....

20   What does it look like to you? ....

21   Please listen to these comments. ....

22   I'm looking forward to finding out about your insights on these issues. ....

23   There will be plenty of time to tune into each other's thinking and sound out ideas. ....

24   Let me illustrate this by … ....

25   I feel really excited about the prospects. ....

B   🔘 **6.01 Watch Zhan giving a product description in his Step 6 presentation. Identify the language he uses to address different representational systems. Complete the gaps.**

When you sit in the car you notice how
(1) .... and (2) .... the seats are.
You can adjust them to make them even more
(3) .... for you, and as you sink in, you
will notice the (4) .... of the real leather.
Take a deep (5) .... and start driving.
You will notice how (6) .... the car is.
Apart from a soft (7) .... and a gentle
(8) ...., you don't (9) ....
very much at all. The car (10) ....
It (11) .... compact and tidy; it has been
designed to make the best use of (12) .... It's a lovely thing to (13) .... at.

C   Categorise the words in the gaps (V, A, K, O or G) according to the representational systems they appeal to.

1 ......   3 ......   5 ......   7 ......   9 ......   11 ......   13 ......
2 ......   4 ......   6 ......   8 ......   10 ......   12 ......

Find Your Voice

Prepare an item from a presentation and address different representational systems. Present this.

Multiple intelligences

A   The theory of multiple intelligences was developed by Dr Howard Gardner, professor of education at Harvard University. Read the text and discuss the two statements below.

1   Everyone has a unique and different mix of intelligence types.

2   It's a good idea to include activities in your presentations that address a mix of intelligences and don't only focus on your personal strengths.

In *Frames of Mind*, I proposed the existence of seven separate human intelligences. **Linguistic intelligence** involves sensitivity to spoken and written language, the ability to learn languages, and the capacity to use language to accomplish certain goals. Lawyers, speakers, writers, poets are among the people with high linguistic intelligence.

Logical-mathematical intelligence involves the capacity to analyse problems logically, carry out mathematical operations, and investigate issues scientifically. Mathematicians, logicians, and scientists exploit logical-mathematical intelligence.

Musical intelligence entails skill in the performance, composition, and appreciation of musical patterns. **Bodily-kinaesthetic intelligence** entails the potential of using one's whole body or parts of the body (like the hand or the mouth) to solve problems or fashion products. Obviously, dancers, actors, and athletes foreground bodily-kinaesthetic intelligence. However, this form of intelligence is also important for craftsmen, surgeons, bench-top scientists, mechanics, and many other technically oriented professionals. **Spatial intelligence** features the potential to recognise and manipulate the patterns of wide space (those used, for instance, by navigators and pilots) as well as the patterns of more confined areas (such as those of importance to sculptors, surgeons, chess players, graphic artists, or architects).

Interpersonal intelligence denotes a person's capacity to understand the intentions, motivations, and desires of other people and consequently, to work effectively with others. Salespeople, teachers, clinicians, religious leaders, political leaders, and actors all need acute interpersonal intelligence. Finally, **intrapersonal intelligence**, involves the capacity to understand oneself, to have an effective working model of oneself – including one's own desires, fears, and capacities – and to use such information effectively in regulating one's own life.

Extract from Frames of Mind: The Theory of Multiple Intelligences

B Highlight the presentation activities in the list a–s that you like or think you could use.
Then, match the presentation activities to 'intelligences' 1–7 below.

a give written handouts ....

b read a poem ....

c pass round objects ....

d use a song as a mantra ....

e demonstrate a product ....

f use a 3D model of a product ....

g vary the pace and use pausing ....

h work with a partner ....

i initiate a discussion ....

j show a film ....

k do a physical activity (e.g. stretching exercises) ....

l solve a problem ....

m do a calculation ....

n use sequencing ....

o play music ....

p let audience walk around ....

q encourage the audience to take notes ....

r give time for personal reflection or individual work ....

s decorate room with posters and pictures ....

1 Linguistic

2 Logical-Mathematical

3 Musical

4 Spatial

5 Bodily-Kinaesthetic

6 Interpersonal

7 Intrapersonal

C Answer the questions below.

1 Assess your personal strengths. Are there other intelligences that you need to consider when you prepare your presentations?

2 Consider the audiences you give presentations to. Are there intelligences that you need to include when you prepare your presentations?

Find Your Voice

Prepare an item from a presentation and address different intelligences. Present this.

Personality types

A Have you heard of Myers-Briggs Type Indicator (MBTI)? If you haven't heard of MBTI, look at the answer key on page 123 and read the description. Answer the questions below.

1 Have you taken the Indicator and do you know your four-letter personality type?

2 Have you done any other kind of personality testing?

3 Why might MBTI be a useful consideration in preparing presentations?

B Read the text and answer the questions on page 82.

In *Type Talk, the sixteen personality types that determine how we live, love and work,* the authors point out that MBTI is a finely tuned instrument that can only be administered by trained individuals but go on to give a framework of statements that readers can agree or disagree with, to informally determine preferences. Here are some of the statements.

If you are an Extravert (E), you probably ...

- know a lot of people, and count many of them among your 'close friends'; you like to include as many people as possible in your activities.
- don't mind reading or having a conversation while the TV or the radio is on in the background; in fact you may well be oblivious to this 'distraction'.
- find telephone calls to be welcome interruptions; you don't hesitate to pick up the phone whenever you have something to tell someone.

If you are an Introvert (I), you probably ...

- enjoy the peace and quiet of having time to yourself; you find your private time too easily invaded and tend to adapt by developing a high power of concentration that can shut out TV, noisy kids or nearby conversations.
- are perceived as 'a great listener' but feel that others take advantage of you.
- wish that you could get your ideas out more forcefully; you resent those who blurt out things you were just about to say.

If you are an Sensor (S), you probably ...

- find most satisfying those jobs that yield some tangible result; as much as you may hate doing housekeeping, you would rather clean your office than think about where your career is headed.
- would rather work with facts and figures than ideas and theories; you like to hear things sequentially instead of randomly.
- think that fantasy is a dirty word; you wonder about people who seem to spend too much time indulging their imagination.

If you are an iNtuitive (N), you probably ...

- believe that 'boring details' is a redundancy.
- find yourself seeking the connections and interrelatedness behind most things rather than accepting them at face value; you're always asking 'What does that mean?'
- tend to give general answers to most questions.

If you are a Thinker (T), you probably ...

- would rather settle a dispute based on what is fair and truthful rather than what will make people happy.
- don't mind making difficult decisions and can't understand why so many people get upset about things that aren't relevant to the issue at hand.
- remember numbers and figures more readily than faces and names.

If you are an Feeler (F), you probably ...

- consider a 'good decision' one that takes others' feeling into account.
- enjoy providing needed services to people although you find that some people take advantage of you.
- are often accused of taking things too personally.

If you are a Judger (J), you probably ...

- are always waiting for others, who never seem to be on time.
- keep lists and use them; if you do something that's not on your list, you may even add it to the list just so you can cross it off.
- are accused of being angry when you're not; you're only stating your opinion.

If you are a Perceiver (P), you probably ...

- love to explore the unknown, even if it's something as simple as a new route home from work.
- have to depend on last-minute spurts of energy to meet deadlines; you usually make the deadline, although you may drive everyone else crazy in the process.
- don't like to be pinned down about most things; you'd rather keep your options open.

1 Which statements do you agree / disagree with?
2 Do you have an idea what your four-letter personality type might be?
3 Why do you think it is useful to know about different personality types?

C Match the personality types 1–8 to the presentation activities a–h in the text.

1 Extraverts   5 Thinking Types
2 Introverts   6 Feeling Types
3 Sensing Types   7 Judging Types
4 Intuitive Types   8 Perceiving Types

PRESENTATION ACTIVITIES

a
- Present options.
- Let the audience make the conclusions.
- Don't press for an immediate decision.
- Give time for a decision and follow up.

b
- Be clear, down-to-earth and practical.
- Give plenty of facts, examples and evidence.
- Keep to the point.
- Give the details.
- Emphasise tangible short-term results.
- Check comprehension.

c
- Be punctual.
- Be well organised.
- Give a plan.
- Begin at the beginning and end at the end.
- Be decisive and give conclusions.
- Emphasise schedules, deadlines and timetables.

d
- Get straight to the point.
- Be brief and concise, but present a complete argument.
- Present clear goals and objectives.
- Define terms and explain what you mean.
- Present all advantages and disadvantages.
- Emphasise rational processes and consequences.
- Use logical arguments.

e
- Talk face-to-face.
- Present to groups and allow interaction.
- Respond to questions and comments.
- Emphasise action.
- Include social interaction.

f
- Be friendly.
- Make the audience feel special.
- Begin with areas of agreement.
- Emphasise human benefits and happiness.
- Use personal examples.
- Give some personal details.

g
- Give the big picture, the broad implications and the long-term possibilities.
- Emphasise concepts and ideas.
- Don't give too many details.
- Inspire.
- Emphasise the unusual and the innovative.
- Expect and welcome ideas, additions and changes.

h
- Give time for reflection both before and after the presentation, possibly by addressing issues in writing.
- Do one-to-one presentations.
- Stick to the business and don't include social interaction.

D 🎦 6.02 Read the brief for the Step 6 presentation on page 86. Watch Zhan and César's short presentation to an audience of male colleagues. What personality types do you think they addressed?

Find Your Voice

- Read the text below and discuss the questions.
  1 Do you already keep an ideas journal, file or notebook?
  2 Do you find the idea 'impractical' and 'incredible' or an 'intelligent course of action'?

- Create a personal *Find Your Voice* ideas book or file. Every time you see or hear something interesting for a presentation, note it down, copy it, cut it out, record it and add it to your book or file. Where can you find ideas and materials? Make a resource checklist. There are some suggestions for resources in the answer key on page 123.

- Write down the following in your *Find Your Voice* book or file.
  1 something you learnt in the last week
  2 something you heard or saw that made a big impression on you
  3 something interesting you read recently

Describe how you could integrate one of these items into a work presentation.

Preventing the loss of good ideas

It doesn't take much thinking to realise that ideas in progress should be caught. Not surprisingly, the greatest minds in history have all realised the wisdom of capturing or documenting their ideas. Creative thinkers ranging from the inventors Thomas Edison, Benjamin Franklin, and Leonardo da Vinci to the novelist Virginia Woolf, the psychologist Carl Jung, and the naturalist Charles Darwin all have used journals and notebooks to record their ideas and inspirations. These people understood that new ideas often come from combining many disparate pieces of information or concepts over an extended period of time. The only effective way to track your ideas and synthesise with them is to document them as soon as they bubble up in your mind.

Capturing an idea makes it more real, more tangible. Whether you act on it within the next six months or the next six years isn't important. Nor is it important whether the people around you deem the idea impractical, or incredible. Simply writing it down for yourself is an intelligent course of action. When you decide to implement the idea at some later date, your written record may be your only source of reliable information.

2 Full presentation

Analysis

A 6.03 Watch Svitlana and Dan's full Step 6 presentation to their work colleagues. As you watch, rate the points in the Feedback form below. If you are working together with a group, discuss your analysis with the group.

Feedback form: Love your audience … not everyone is like you					
	Poor	OK	Good	Wow!	Comments
Jump start					
Issues					
Recommendation					
Benefits					
Evidence					
Finish with a bang					
Teamwork					

B 6.03 Watch again. Do the presenters use any 'love your audience' activities or language?

Preparation and presentation

A   Read the brief and prepare your own presentation.

Full presentation practice: Team presentation

Subject and structure

This is a team presentation. Find a partner to prepare and do the presentation with. You should persuade your audience to do something out of the ordinary. Here are some suggestions but you can be as imaginative and crazy as you wish.

- do a bungee jump next week and everyone pays for the jump himself / herself
- audition for the next reality TV series
- have a karaoke machine in the company canteen
- have a once a month 'creativity day' in your organisation
- do a 100km trek across a desert for charity

Use this framework:

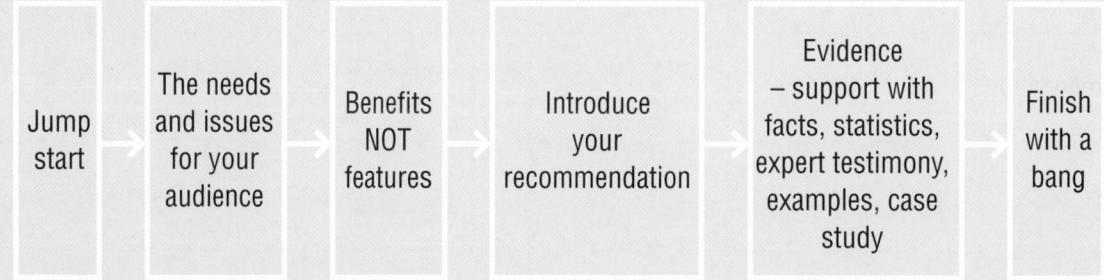

Jump start → The needs and issues for your audience → Benefits NOT features → Introduce your recommendation → Evidence – support with facts, statistics, expert testimony, examples, case study → Finish with a bang

Your audience

Your colleagues

Your targets

- To work effectively as a team
- To convince and persuade your audience you have the right vision
- To love your audience
- And last, but no means least, to have a lot of fun!

B   Give your full presentation.

Feedback and targets

A   If you're working in a group, analyse each others' presentations, using the Feedback form below. If you're working alone, record yourself and analyse your own performance.

Feedback form: Love your audience … not everyone is like you					
	Poor	**OK**	**Good**	**Wow!**	**Comments**
Jump start					
Issues					
Recommendation					
Benefits					
Evidence					
Finish with a bang					
Teamwork					
'Love your audience' activities					

Presentations diary

B   Look back at your feedback on your Step 6 presentation and, if possible, watch your presentation again. Now read 1–4 below and write your diary for Step 6.

1   Did your presentation take into account different personality types and intelligences?
2   List two things that you could have done to improve teamwork.
3   Set yourself two targets for your next full presentation.
4   List three items you added or will add to your *Find Your Voice* ideas book or file.

Presentations forum

C   Start a presentation forum in your organisation. Choose five people to invite to your forum. Fix a date and time for the first meeting. Decide on the first presentation topic.

- Meet regularly to discuss presentations.
- Use the presentation briefs in this book.
- Prepare real work presentations.
- Use the feedback forms in this book.
- Design in-house analysis forms.
- Invite guest presenters.
- Invite a presentations trainer or coach.
- Create a *Find Your Voice* culture.

Step 7 Questions are a big opportunity, aren't they?

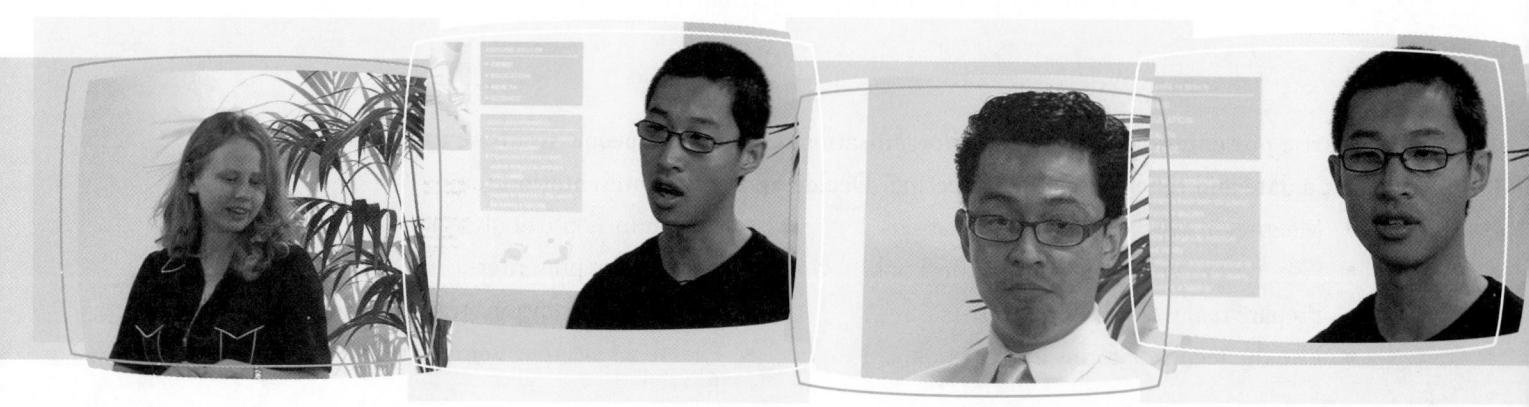

1 Questions

Introduction

A **Discuss the questions below.**

1 Why do people ask questions during a presentation?

2 What are the advantages in opening up a dialogue?

3 What are the disadvantages?

4 When do you invite questions? Why?

B **Which of the following statements do you agree or disagree with? Why?**

When do you take questions?

1 For me it's a big enough problem to get through the presentation and to do it in English. I really don't want to worry about understanding and answering questions on top of everything else. I ask the audience to leave the questions until the end or even to write me an email afterwards. That gives me more time to think about the answers.

2 I have to do a lot of project proposal presentations and it's important that my audiences understand the whole argumentation and the background to the proposal before they ask questions. An interactive presentation would simply disturb the flow of the arguments. If there is a long question and answer session though, I always make another quick summary and conclusion so that the main message isn't lost. I believe this gives a better sense of closure too.

3 At the beginning of the presentation I make it clear that I'll take about three or four questions at the end of every point. I move on to the next point as soon as I've answered about four questions. This lets me manage and control the presentation and I can keep to my timing. It also makes the audience really concentrate on asking relevant and clear questions.

4 If you want to allow questions during your presentation, you have to be really well-prepared. You have to be able to come back to your structure and get things back on track. Another advantage of good preparation is that you can refer the question forward to a later point in the presentation if this is in your structure. You don't waste time then and the audience can see how well you are managing the presentation. It creates a good impression.

5 Actually, I much prefer to have lots of questions in the presentation, even when the presentation is in English. I think it suits my personality much better as I can talk with people and not talk at them – a dialogue rather than a monologue. It's all about building up a relationship and that's the most important thing in my line of business.

6 If I'm presenting in English to a multicultural audience and they all have different levels of English, I think it is absolutely vital to allow questions at any time. There could be things that people simply don't understand and that it's important to clarify as soon as possible. If I didn't do this, I could get to the conclusion and people wouldn't understand it.

Reporting questions

Delivery: Questions as statements

A You can simply repeat a question, using the same words in the same order, but using falling intonation. The question then becomes a statement. Work with a partner. Take turns to be the questioner and the presenter.

Questioner: Ask questions 1–10. Use a rising tone (↗) at the end of each *Yes / No* question and a falling tone (↘) at the end of each *Wh-* question.

Presenter: Repeat questions 1–10. Use a falling tone (↘) at the end of each question.

Change roles and do the exercise again.

1 What are the problems?
2 How should we go about this?
3 Does your CEO go along with this?
4 What are the risks?
5 Can we justify the expenditure?
6 Why did you reject option A?
7 Is there any other solution?
8 Do you envisage any future for ABC technology?
9 What are the reasons we were so successful in Vietnam and not in Malaysia?
10 Do our competitors have a similar product?

Grammar: Reported questions

Yes / No questions	Wh- questions
Direct *Are you planning any further changes?* *Did you approve that decision?*	**Direct** *What further changes are you planning?* *Why did you approve that decision?*
Indirect *He asked if we're planning any further changes.* *She asked whether I approved that decision.*	**Indirect** *He asked what further changes we're planning.* *She asked why I approved that decision.*

Notes

- Changes to word order
- Use of *if / whether* in *Yes / No* questions and repetition of question words (*where, why, how,* etc.) in *wh-* questions
- When we report questions in presentations, the tense usually stays the same because the information in the question is still true.

B **Change the direct questions below into reported questions.**

1 What was the accident rate last year?

You asked ....

2 Why did you respond in that way?

You asked ....

3 How many clients did we handle last year?

You asked ....

4 Do you foresee any change in the situation?

You asked ....

5 Can the market sustain this growth rate?

You asked ....

6 What is your pricing structure?

You asked ....

7 Have you had any experience of this with other clients?

You asked ....

8 When exactly did the auditors come?

You asked ....

Paraphrasing

C **You can clarify meaning, gain thinking time and share the question with the whole audience by paraphrasing the question. Paraphrasing also has the following advantages.**

1 Making the question less personal by avoiding the repetition of *I, you, we*, etc.

Did you do any market research? → *The question is about market research.*

2 Making a question less negative by changing negative vocabulary into more neutral or positive vocabulary.

When did you discover this strategy was a disaster? → *So you are asking when we knew this strategy wasn't working as well as expected.*

Think of ways to paraphrase questions 1–8 below. Use one of these introductory phrases.

You would like to know …	If I understand the question correctly, you would like to know …
So you are asking … So, your question is about … The question is about …	

1 Why did the project fail?

2 Do you have experience at all in this field?

3 Are you really saying that we should go ahead with this?

4 Are there more disadvantages than the ones you mentioned?

5 How expensive is it?

6 Is your company really in a position to …?

7 Do you have the finances in place?

8 Do you think that your figures are accurate?

2 Answers

Answering strategies

A Choose the best response (a, b or c) for questions 1–8. Then define the question and the strategy the presenter uses to answer each question. Check your answers on page 124.

1 **When you say 'pay freeze', what do you mean exactly?**
   a I don't know.
   b So, you're asking me about the worsening of your employment conditions.
   c Let me put it in another way, …

2 **Why did you spend so much money on marketing? What was the budget for the spring catalogue? And what is the total budget for this year?**
   a What is your question exactly?
   b You've raised three points there. Let me take them one by one. First, the marketing budget.
   c So, you want to know how much money we spent. Well, that's a difficult question.

3 **It's too expensive.**
   a What's your question exactly?
   b So, you're asking me about pricing structure.
   c No, it's not.

4 **I'm really not happy with the way you went about this. What went wrong?**
   a So, you're asking about what errors we have identified in the system.
   b I'm sorry you're not happy.
   c Nothing went wrong actually.

5 **Don't you agree that the second option is actually better?**
   a No, I don't.
   b So, you would like me to run through the advantages of the second option in more detail.
   c You're asking me whether I agree with you or not.

6 **I'd like to ask a question about your third option.**
   a I'll be addressing that point later in my presentation.
   b That's not relevant at the moment.
   c I don't want to answer that now.

7 **So, that's the engineering plan, but what about the budget?**
   a The budget's not my job.
   b I don't know anything about money.
   c Our financial director Michael Braun is probably the best person to answer that, Michael?

8 **Could you tell me about your company's differential edge?**
   a No, I can't understand you.
   b I didn't get that. Could you repeat your question in other words?
   c Sorry, no, my English is not good enough.

Q&A analysis

A   7.01 Watch Svitlana, Zhan and César answering questions during their Step 7 presentations. What strategies do they use to answer the questions?

B   Look at the transcripts of the questions and answers on page 125. Match the transcript 1–10 in the answer key with the correct analysis of the question and strategy a–j below.

a   The presenter paraphrases by using the original wording of the question and makes it clear he / she can't answer the question.

b   The questioner interrupts and uses a sequence of questions. The presenter accepts the question and answers it non-defensively even though he / she is at a critical point in the presentation. The presenter paraphrases and answers the first question. He / She asks for repetition of the second question. (If the second question was difficult, the presenter might be lucky as the questioner could have forgotten the second or even third question!)

c   The questioner uses a sequence of questions. The presenter paraphrases and answers the second question. The questioner is responsible for the sequence and the presenter can't be expected to remember the whole sequence. The presenter clearly gives the answer to the whole audience.

d   The presenter paraphrases the question. He / She switches the emphasis from 'convincing' to 'agreeing' in the paraphrase.

e   The presenter paraphrases by using the original wording of the question and answers it by referring back to an earlier point.

f   The questioner uses a sequence of questions. The presenter separates the questions and points out that there are two questions. He / She paraphrases and answers both fully.

g   The presenter paraphrases the question and answers it very briefly but goes on to point out that the question is not relevant.

h   The presenter paraphrases and asks for clarification. He / She then refers the question forward to a later point in the presentation, demonstrating effective management of the presentation.

i   The presenter paraphrases and takes the question in the direction the presenter feels is necessary. He / She gives himself / herself thinking time with the paraphrase and some standard phrases.

j   The presenter paraphrases and uses more positive vocabulary in the paraphrase.

Hidden meanings

A **Analyse these questions, considering the definitions you have examined in this step.**

1 I want to take you up on your point about France going into recession. I don't think we're prepared for this.

2 Yes, that's all very well, but what are the reasons for your very high prices?

3 I'm not happy!

4 I'm not convinced. Can you give me an example of a company where such an approach is working?

5 So, what are your prices? We don't know your customers. What is your experience?

6 Do you agree that we are going into recession and you will therefore have to reduce your prices?

7 Are you sure these figures are accurate?

8 Do you really expect us to believe that you represent the best value on the market?

9 If I understand you correctly, you said you have the highest prices on the market?

10 How does your company compare with XYZ in terms of pricing?

11 How do you justify using XYZ graphics company?

12 Do you honestly expect us to believe that you are the best on the market?

13 Could you tell me what you mean by 'incentive scheme'?

14 What research did you do exactly? We're not very happy with what you did last time.

B **Questioners don't always ask clear questions and the key issue isn't always explicitly stated. Listening, analysis, paraphrasing and clarifying can help the presenter to find the key issue behind a question. Match the possible hidden questions / issues a–n to questions 1–14 in exercise A.**

a We've spoken to XYZ and we know their prices. ....

b What plans do you have? ....

c Have you changed anything since last time? ....

d What are your credentials? ....

e The key issue could be anything as this is just an emotional statement. This needs clarification before the presenter gets defensive or sidetracks on an irrelevant issue. ....

f Are you good value for money? Can you tell me about your experience and back up your pricing strategy? What are your credentials? ....

g Have you checked these figures carefully? ....

h A request for clarification or a question about pricing structure? ....

i What's the pricing structure? Are we getting good value for money? ....

j What are XYZ graphics company's credentials? ....

k You're using jargon that I can't understand. ....

l How can I be sure that this is a good strategy? ....

m Are we getting good value for money? Tell me about what I get for my money. ....

n Are we paying too much at the present time? ....

Check in the answer key on page 126.

Find Your Voice

A Read the brief for the full Step 7 presentation on page 97. Choose the project you will present. Alternatively, take a real work or study presentation. Then, prepare fifteen questions that could be asked during this presentation, which fit into the categories below.

Questions (1–5) I expect and can definitely answer

1 ....
2 ....
3 ....
4 ....
5 ....

Questions (6–10) I would expect but would find difficult to answer

6 ....
7 ....
8 ....
9 ....
10 ....

Questions (11–15) I wouldn't want someone to ask and would find very difficult to answer

11 ....
12 ....
13 ....
14 ....
15 ....

B Now prepare responses to all fifteen questions above.

C Get into small groups. One person in the group is a presenter.

Presenter: Make a photocopy of the fifteen questions you prepared in A and give a copy to each person in your group. Stand in front of the group. Give the last sentence of your presentation and invite questions.

- Listen carefully to each question.
- Analyse the question.
- Paraphrase each question defining the key issue.
- Answer in a neutral and non-defensive manner.

Now do a quick summary and / or conclusion and thank the audience.

Rest of group: Select questions from all three categories and ask the presenter your questions.

After the exercise, assess:
- if the presenter was able to answer all questions.
- if the presenter answered all questions neutrally.

3 Full presentation

Analysis

A   7.02 Watch César's Step 7 presentation. As you watch, rate the points in the Feedback form below. If you are working together with a group, discuss your analysis with the group.

Feedback form: Questions are a big opportunity, aren't they?					
	Poor	OK	Good	Wow!	Comments
Start					
Signposting					
Structure					
Delivery					
Visual aids					
Techniques					
Positive and dramatic					
Love the audience					
Dealing with questions					
Finish					
Project sold?					

Preparation and presentation

A   Read the brief and prepare your own presentation.

Full presentation practice: My project

Subject and structure
- a work related project
- a project for your country or organisation

You need to 'sell' the project.

Choose one of the frameworks already discussed or experiment with your own structure, bearing in mind it should be simple, logical and clear. Your ideas should flow easily. State in your introduction that you are willing to take questions at any time during the presentation.

Your audience

A multinational company or organisation whose working language is English. The audience consists of members of the Board and senior management. They come from all over the world and the language level ranges from an intermediate to native speaker level.

Your targets
- To 'sell' yourself, your company or organisation, and your project
- To have a well structured presentation
- To give an interactive presentation whilst maintaining a clear structure and timing
- To answer all questions neutrally and non-defensively
- To use as full a range of techniques as possible

B   Give your full presentation.

Feedback and targets

A   If you're working in a group, analyse each others' presentations, using the Feedback form.
If you're working alone, record yourself and analyse your own performance.

Feedback form: Questions are a big opportunity, aren't they?					
	Poor	**OK**	**Good**	**Wow!**	**Comments**
Start					
Signposting					
Structure					
Delivery					
Visual aids					
Techniques					
Positive and dramatic					
Love the audience					
Dealing with questions					
Finish					
Project sold?					

Presentations diary

B   Look back at your feedback on your Step 7 presentation and, if possible, watch your presentation
again. Now read 1–4 below and write your diary for Step 7.

1   How did you react to the questions?

2   Did the questions add to the presentation?

3   Was the structure of your presentation clear?

4   Describe the 'relationship' between yourself and your audience.

C   Now, go back through all your presentation diaries in this book.

1   Select five things that stand out for you and / or five things you want to research further.

2   Select five points where you definitely 'found your voice'.

3   Select five targets you achieved.

4   Write five targets for your future presentations in English.

D   7.02 Now watch Dan, Svitlana, Zhan and César's comments and reflections after they finished
the presentations training.

Answer key and video script

Introduction

A 🔘 **0.01 Dan**

Hi, my name is Dan. Actually my real name is Danupol Aphichitsakul, but it's very long so everyone calls me Dan. I'm a student at Brookes, I'm studying publishing as a Master degree course and I'm from Bangkok, Thailand.

I need to take the presentation course in English because … my work involve a lot with English people and English contexts so because I plan to work in an international company in Thailand, and … I think actually in my, you know, in my field of job, my field of work is publishing, you need to make a lot of presentation and a kind of selling your ideas because, the board of committees they have lots of proposals but what's important for them when they make a decision is through the presentation of your…

I think the obstacle, the main obstacles are the different you know, different mentalities between you know, different people from different countries because sometimes, like, when we talk to the foreign people we need to kind of change our way of saying things or doing things, you know, to make them, to persuade them to, to … make it more, you know, accessible for them sometimes, it's really hard to see who's for what, you know. For the presentation in English I think I need to be more confident and you know, look more professional and be more sharp. You know when you do a presentation because I think that's what people expect from you, kind of confidence in yourself, why, rather in my language it's more like a friendly … and … because I think we come from the same country, so we kind of takes things more easy …

1 Dan is a student at Brookes [University]. He's studying for a Masters in publishing.
2 He's from Bangkok, Thailand.
3 He plans to work for an international company in Thailand and his work involves working with English people in English contexts. In publishing you need to make a lot of presentations and sell your ideas to the Board.
4 You have to change the way you say and do things to make it more accessible for a foreign audience.
5 He wants to be more confident, professional and sharp.

A 🔘 **0.02 Svitlana**

My name is Svitlana. I'm originally from Ukraine. I've been in Oxford for around two years, and I'm working as a guide at the Bodleian Library in Oxford.

I thought it would be important for me, not so much for my job as a guide in the library, which is also important I think, but because I'm doing my PhD in Economics, I'm presenting in front of a committee … it's always stressful, so I thought it would help

me to gain some confidence and I hoped I would learn a few new techniques to improve my presentations.

It is important for me … because I'm actually going to look for a job in management and that's where you actually have to do presentations almost every day, and they must be of a very high quality, and that's why, though I'm very happy with the job I'm doing now, when I, when I move on to, to the next job, I thought I would better gain my skills before that.

It feels different when you present in English, and it is difficult because first I've got a very strong accent, and I used to speak very fast and it's why for people it is very, very difficult to understand me here. When I moved here first, it was a disaster because nobody could understand me, I couldn't understand other people, and learning how to present, it would help even in a daily life to make myself more clear to other people.

For my first presentation, I was working on structurising it and I thought that if I could do it in English, I then would be able to do it in Russian as well, so, that's why I'm looking forward and very excited about how it's going to be, because I thought I really understood what I studied and I could implement the structure into my presentation, so I really want to see the feedback of audience to see what they think of my presentation.

1 She's originally from Ukraine.
2 She is living in Oxford and working as a guide in the Bodleian library.
3 She thinks it will be useful for her phD in Economics. She would like to gain more confidence and learn some new techniques. She's going to look for a job in management and you have to do high quality presentations almost every day.
4 She's got a very strong accent and used to speak very fast. She thinks people find it difficult to understand her.
5 She wants to be clearer and implement a good structure to her presentations and to get feedback from her audience.

A 🔘 **0.03 Zhan**

My name's Zhan Su. I was born in China but I'm now living in England. I'm a PhD student at the University of Oxford. I study statistical genetics at the statistics department.

It's important for me to take the course in English because English is the scientific language, so if we're going to present our ideas it will just be, most of the time it'll be in English.

1 He was born in China but he's now living in England.
2 He's a phD student at the University of Oxford, studying statistical genetics.
3 English is the scientific language and most of the time you have to present in English.

A 🎧 **0.04 César**

My name is César Ramirez and I am from Mexico and I am a lawyer working for an international law firm.

Well, this course is particularly important because as part of my everyday activities I have to give presentations to clients or to other colleagues or to just you know people in general, about particular aspects of what we do, or the sort of things that we look at when we engage in litigation or when we study a case.

I'm hoping to achieve a very, a much better understanding of how to give more effective presentations and how to be more confident in what I say, how I say it, and how it can be more effective, you know, in the way I'm saying it, and also to be able to say things in a more just confident way as opposed to be, you know, always very nervous about it and always, like, panicking.

It was up until about six years ago that I actually started to speak English. Before I'd, you know, I had been educated in Spanish, I had been, you know, trained in Spanish, and my mind was used to speaking Spanish and thinking in Spanish, so when you give presentations, obviously native speakers always make use of the, you know, the sorts of education and training that they received from a very early age, and these resources obviously I, I lack in, because I wasn't educated in, in English, so the fact of the course is actually helping me to be able to you know, understand the way native speakers would give a presentation effectively, and where maybe they would place more emphasis or where they would actually pause, and where they would actually be more emphatic.

1 César's from Mexico.
2 He's a lawyer, working for an international law firm.
3 As part of his everyday activities, he has to give presentations to clients and colleagues.
4 He wants to achieve a much better understanding of how to give an effective presentation and how to be more confident.
5 He doesn't have the same resources as a native speaker who was educated in English, so he doesn't automatically know how to emphasise, pause, or be more emphatic.

Step 1 Lay solid foundations

1 The start

Attention curve

A The chart below shows what the curve looks like for an average presentation.

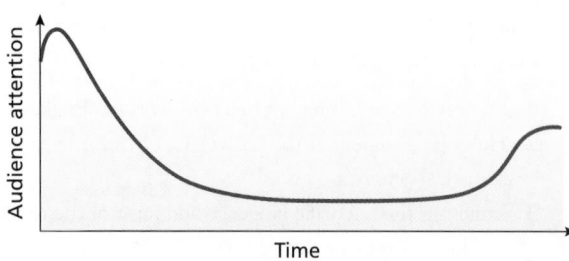

B Most listeners tend to remember most easily information given at the 'start' and 'finish' and these are two important sections of a presentation. The first items are referred to as 'primacy' and the last items as 'recency' and these are easier to recall than items in the middle of a presentation. This is called the 'serial position effect' which occurs in all kinds of learning and presentation. The graph below demonstrates the serial position effect.

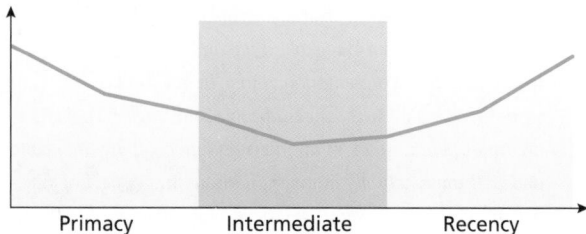

There is a parallel between the audience attention listening curve and the serial position effect graph.

Who, why, what, how

A Who is the presenter? **2, 6**
Why are we all here? **1**
What is he going to talk about? **3, 4**
How is he going to organise the presentation? **5, 7, 8**

C
1 who	10 what	19 how
2 why	11 why	20 how
3 what	12 how	21 what
4 who	13 how	22 why
5 how	14 why	23 why
6 who	15 who	24 how
7 why	16 how	25 why
8 what	17 how	26 who
9 what	18 who	

D 🎧 **1.01 César**

Good afternoon everyone. Thank you very much for coming to my presentation. Let me introduce myself. I am César Ramirez and I am a lawyer working for an international law firm. Today I would like to give you a general overview of the growing and really broad area of trademark law. So I'll be addressing three main points, and the first one is going to be 'what'. What we protect when we say 'trademarks' and what we actually mean by the word 'trademark'. The second point will be why we care about trademarks and why we should be concerned with trademarks. And finally, the last point is how we protect trademarks, how the law is concerned with trademarks, how courts and judges protect trademarks.

4 Let me introduce myself. I am … I am a ….

7 Today I would like to give you a general overview of …

9 So, I'll be addressing three main points and the first one is going to be … The second point will be …
And finally the last point is …

1.02 Zhan

Morning everyone. I'm Zhan Su. I'm a statistics department PhD student at the University of Oxford and today, I'm going to tell you a little bit about my research. I'm going to briefly tell you what I do, briefly tell you how I do it and finally I'm going to tell you why I do it. The presentation should last about five minutes and I'm happy to take any questions after that.

26 Morning everyone. I'm … I'm a … at …

22 Today, I'm going to tell you …

12 The presentation should last about five minutes.

17 I'm happy to take any questions after that.

Grammar

A 1.03 Dan

Hi everyone. Today I would like to be talking about an overview of the Russian book market. Firstly, I'll go through some general info about the, you know, the country itself. Then, I'll move on to the economy and the politics side and then I'd like to go into details with the educational market and the trade publishing.

1 'll go through   2 'll move on   3 'd like to

1.04 Svitlana

Dear members of the committee. I'm delighted to be with you here today. My name is Svitlana and the subject of my research is the deviant behaviour of economic agents in your emerging economies. Today I'm going to tell you why I chose this topic and how you can benefit from my research. I will start by telling you what we consider to be a deviant behaviour in economics. I will move on to giving you a few examples.

4 'm going to   5 will start   6 will move on

1 They use *will, would like* and *going to.*

2 It's a good idea to use a variety of forms to avoid monotony and to increase interest at the start.

B Suggestions

1 Firstly, I'll give the background to the project. Then, I'm going to tell you about the present situation and then I'd like to show the future changes.

2 In my first point I'd like to show you the structure of the department, my second point is going to be our work procedures and my third point will be suggestions for greater efficiency.

---

3 I'd like to develop three main points. Firstly, I'll give a general overview. Secondly, I'm going to move on to specifics and thirdly, I'll describe the overall changes.

2 The finish

Signal, summary, conclusion, closing remarks

A 1 Giving a presentation can be stressful and giving a presentation in another language can be even more stressful. One effect of this is that presenters often feel relieved when they get to the finish of the main part and they simply don't go through all or any of the steps at the end. Presenters sometimes fail to summarise or confuse summary and conclusion and give conclusions during the summary. This means the message of the presentation can become unclear or lost.

2 Every presentation has some kind of conclusion. Even if you are giving information, you want the audience to know and understand more by the end of the presentation. This should be explicit and linked to the 'why' at the 'start'.

B					
1	Sig	8	Conc	15	CR
2	Sum	9	Sig	16	Sum
3	CR	10	Sum	17	Conc
4	Sum	11	Sum	18	CR
5	CR	12	Conc	19	Sum
6	Conc	13	Conc	20	Conc
7	Sum	14	Sig		

Grammar

A 1.05 César

So, this third point brings me to the end of my presentation. To summarise, we've looked at what a trade mark is and its definition. We've looked at why we protect trademarks and why we are concerned with them, and thirdly we've looked at how we protect them. So, I hope and I trust that this has given you a really good insight into what trade mark law is and that it might be thought-provoking for you.

1 Present perfect

2 It is effective as the use of the present perfect indicates the content of the presentation is connected to the present, i.e. the summary and conclusion. Its use in a summary can be more dramatic than the use of the past simple.

3 Yes

4 Yes, it was simple and uncomplicated. The conclusion – to make us think about trademark law – was clear and led directly from the summary.

B

1	envied	11	have / changed
2	was	12	have been
3	made	13	have made
4	set	14	have allocated
5	appointed	15	have introduced
6	meant	16	has become
7	didn't attend	17	have started
8	was	18	have found
9	wasted	19	had
10	didn't have	20	have seen

3 Structuring

Signposting

A  1.06 **Dan**

It's helping my language, my English because I have a structure there and what I need to put in. I just look at the structures and put something in. And when I speak I feel more confident because I know what is next and what to expect … I tend to make less mistakes because I know what to expect – expect this kind of structures and signposting tell me what will be next.

1 Structuring helps Dan because he knows what comes next and what to expect.

B  1.07 **Svitlana**

<u>So, let's start with my presentation</u>. <u>I would like to begin by</u> emphasising the importance of a deviant behaviour of economic agents and the impact it has on our lives. Let's face it, all of us feel deviant to some extent in different situations and because of that we can behave inadequately and even cause distress to other people. The same thing happens in economics when people do things that are illegal, abnormal or just atypical. Deviant behaviour is widely acknowledged in psychology, criminology and sociology, but not in economics where it happens very often indeed. <u>Let me move on to</u> giving you a few examples. We would all agree that committing suicide, killings, violations of social norms is considered abnormal or deviant. <u>This leads me to a point</u> that bribing a judge to get a satisfactory outcome of the trial, corrupting the teachers to get a better mark at the exam is a deviant behaviour too, which happens in economics almost on a daily basis. <u>Let's now turn</u> to what we consider to be a deviant behaviour in economics. As a deviant behaviour in economics we consider corruption and all sorts of economic crime, the most common of which is tax fraud. <u>Now, what about</u> positive deviations? They do exist as well and though sometimes they can present themselves as negative deviations, later on they can become forward-pushing changes, especially in re-emerging economies. That is why identifying the kinds of deviations and studying them is a necessary step in building a more just and successful society.

 1.08 **Zhan**

<u>So, first of all</u>, what is it I do? So, I work in a field called mathematical genetics and essentially what we do is trying to locate those parts of our genome, those parts of our DNA that causes disease. So, if you imagine our bodies to be machines, then like any other machine our bodies are prone to break down. So, some of that is because we haven't been taking care of it very well. So, for example, bad diet, lack of exercise, but some of the reasons are because our bodies is not built very well and the reason why that is, is because there are faults in our DNA, our DNA are the blueprints to our bodies, to the machines. So, what we do is try to locate those parts of our DNA that causes these diseases. So, I've just listed some of those diseases that you might recognise. This whole topic is quite topical, quite relevant at the moment because a couple of days ago there was an article on BBC news about obesity and what that was about is that they found an obesity gene that means that patients who have this gene is more likely to have obesity irrespective of their lifestyle and so that's exactly what we do. We're trying to locate genes such as the obesity gene. So, that's pretty much what I do <u>and this is</u> how I do it. So, in a very kind of brief simplistic view of what we do is we analyse two sets of genetic data. The first set of genetic data comes from patients that carry a disease that we are interested in. So, for example, obesity. The second set of genetic data comes from patients that don't carry the disease. So, they're patients who, they're people who don't have obesity and we analyse the two together and hopefully what we find is that in the obesity data set they all carry a set of genes that are not found in the other data set where people don't have obesity. This is a very, very simple view. We're talking about huge amounts of data and we're using statistics to kind of model, analyse this data. So, that's why we're in the statistics department. <u>So, that was</u> how I do it <u>and finally</u> why, OK. So, we're doing this because by locating the genetic causes of certain diseases, we're better understanding the diseases and eventually, that will hopefully lead to a cure or at least prevention for these diseases. So, for example, pharmaceutical companies by knowing where the obesity gene is, will be able to develop drugs that negates the effect of this gene. So, hopefully, in the future there might be a drug that cures obesity or at least prevents it and so that is why we do it. <u>So, that's pretty much</u> the what, the how and the why.

Svitlana

2 I would like to begin by …
3 Let's turn now to …
4 Let's start with my presentation.
7 Now, what about …?
8 Let me move on to …
11 This leads me to a point …

Zhan

5   So, first of all …

15   So, that's pretty much …

16   and this is …

18   So, that was …

22   And finally …

Note: Zhan often uses a singular verb form with a plural noun. This is Chinese interference. He should have said:

… *our bodies are not built very well* (not … *our bodies is not built very well*)

… *our DNA is the blueprints to our bodies* (not … *our DNA are the blueprints to our bodies*)

… *patients who have this gene are more likely to have obesity* (not … *patients who have this gene is more likely to have obesity*)

… *will be able to develop drugs that negate the effect of this gene.* (not … *will be able to develop drugs that negates the effect of this gene.*)

C   Signposts are important because they help the presenter structure and shape the content and guide the audience through the presentation.

Delivery: Pausing

A 🔊 1.09 **Svitlana**

I realized that of course, obviously there was still room for improvement so my goal for the next presentation was to improve a little bit signposting and pausing because sometimes the pausing they bring even more attention from audience than not pausing. Basically when you speak very fast, it is difficult for people to follow, so that was my goal, which I partly achieved in the second presentation. I felt that I was getting more confident with using English and I was not afraid of using words that I do not use in daily life.

Pausing helps the audience to follow the presentation especially when the presenter tends to speak fast.

B 🔊 1.10 **César**

I can't think of any particular word or any particular phrase or any particular you know, way of saying that I should actually improve, but I suppose the most important thing about this course and that, you know, I've learnt, has been to be able to pause and to be able to breathe and to be able to just listen to myself a bit before moving on to the next point, you know, that I want to address. And I suppose it's something I don't do because as I said, you know, being a Spanish native speaker, we don't pause, we just keep talking and talking because ideas and words just flow, and they just keep coming into your mind, so I suppose you never stop to think about what you want to say. Whereas in English I suppose, because I'm in front of an audience, and because they're all native speakers, and because I am not, that

makes me anxious and that makes me think twice before saying it, as opposed to when you're a native speaker, you just utter words out, you just blurt them out and, you know, they just flow very naturally, so I can't really think of a specific example of a particular word for example, or things like that, that I would like to, you know, just be aware of and be able to have it as a target, but I suppose it's little things like pausing, it's little things that being more, you know, sign posting, being, you know, more, I suppose, clearer about what I'm going to do next. I suppose this is one of the things which I haven't actually, which I didn't actually know, and which I've learned.

1   Breathing and listening to himself.

2   They help a non-native speaker think about what to say in front of native speaker audience. César says 'he can listen to himself' when he breathes and pauses.

3   Pausing and breathing help to pace and signpost a presentation bringing attention to key points and new directions in a presentation. Both techniques can also help to calm nerves.

4   A presentation is essentially a monologue and the presenter feels a need to fill in silence which feels unnatural to him / her.

4   Full presentation

🔊 1.11 **César**

Good afternoon everyone. Thank you very much for coming to my presentation. Let me introduce myself. I am César Ramirez, and I am a lawyer working for an international law firm. Today I would like to give you a general overview of the growing and really broad area of trademark law. So I'll be addressing three main points, and the first one is going to be 'what'. What we protect when we say 'trademarks' and what we actually mean by the word 'trademark'. The second point will be why we care about trademarks and why we should be concerned with trademarks. And finally, the last point is how we protect trademarks, how the law is concerned with trademarks, and how courts and judges protect trademarks. Excuse me.

So let me just turn to my first point. What a trademark is, is a very important question because that will determine whether or not we've got a claim and we've got a right. So the first thing to note is that a trademark is any sign that could be used by a trader to identify his or her goods from other traders' and at the same time to distinguish those goods from the goods of other traders. The concept of a sign has not always been the same, though. It's been changing over time and is actually being broadened and broadened as time goes by. So in the beginning for example, a trademark would just be used as an identifier. Nowadays, for example, a trademark can be used, for example as a general appearance, as the persona, as the image, etc. of a general company. So the concept has actually been evolving and growing very, very steadily and fast over the past decades.

The second question is 'Why we protect trademarks?' and over here I would like to draw your attention to the fact … and to the actual rationale behind the protection and, at the same time, I would like to talk about two main points here. The first one is consumers, while the second one is the information. So the reason why we protect trademarks is because they are supposed to be carriers of information that tell the consumer where the goods come from and at the same time, they reassure the consumer that the goods they are buying, he or she is buying, come from the same undertaking, from the same origin and is a constant quality. So rather than me going into a supermarket and trying to find out whether or not those goods are actually of a good quality, the quality I expect, I can just use the trademark, and always expect the same quality with confidence. So that is the rationale of the main protection for trademarks.

Finally, this point brings me to my second, to my third point, which is … so and this brings me to my third point, and last point, which is, how we protect trademarks, and at this point I would like to draw your attention to the fact that there is a very basic and, at the same time, very important principle in trademark law which is 'confusion'. We protect trademarks to the extent that there is confusion. What sort of confusion? It's consumer confusion, and that is … not only the consumer is confused as to the origin of the goods but also, if the consumer is confused, as to the fact that the goods may be affiliated or could be endorsed or sponsored by the producer.

So this third point brings me to the end of my presentation. To summarise, we've looked at what a trademark is and its definition. We've looked at why we protect trademarks and why we are concerned with them, and thirdly we've looked at how we protect them. So, I hope and I trust that this has given you a really good insight into what trademark law is and that it might be thought-provoking for you. Thank you very much for listening and if you've got any questions, please feel free to ask.

Step 2 Connect with your audience

1 Jump start
Introduction

B 1 Meet the People
   2 WIIFM
   3 Enrolment questions
   4 Quotations
   5 Shocking statement or startling statistic
   6 Expert testimony or historical evidence
   7 Question and answer

C 1 a 2 c 3 e 4 b 5 d 6 e and g 7 f

Techniques: WIIFM

B 1 c   2 a

Techniques: Quotations

C 🔘 2.01 **Svitlana**

Good afternoon ladies and gentlemen. I'm delighted to be here with you today. My name is Svitlana and the goal of my presentation is to bring you up to date with the current political situation in Ukraine. As a famous German philosopher Friedrich Nietzsche said once, 'Madness is rarer in individuals, but in groups, political parties, nations, it's the rule' and that's apparently what happened in Ukraine during the Orange Revolution in December 2004, January 2005. Today I'm going to tell you why this topic started to interest me …

Techniques: Shocking statement or statistic

E 🔘 2.02 **César**

Right, may I just explain a bit? Trademark law has never cared about the psychological functions of trademark. Do you know what I mean? Trademark law has always … been concerned to the protection of identification of a product – not if a mark gives me satisfaction because it's associated with top models or because it's associated with Michael Jordon, for example when he sells his trainers. It's never been concerned about that. So that's a very, very … trademark lawyers who understand that are very important, very, you know, far-reaching statement. Do you know what I mean? Maybe it doesn't cause the same impact, you know, you may not be experts, but if a lawyer was listening to me, a trademark lawyer, he would say he's talking rubbish or … what's he on about …?

1 Trademark law has never been concerned with the psychological functions of a trademark.
2 They would find it a far-reaching statement and would wonder what he was talking about.

🔘 2.03 **César**

The protection of trademark law has been recently conceded to be the protection of the psychologcal functions of trademarks. In this presentation about trademark law I would like to give you an overview of what trademark law is about …

Techniques: Combining 'jump start' techniques

E 🔘 2.04 **Dan**

Hi everyone. Thank you for coming to the seminar today. The seminar today is about the independent bookshop. So, I would like to start with a – you know – a question. Do you know how many independent bookshops in Britain has closed in the last five months? Anyone? (ten, fifteen). That's a good number. It's around 35. That's according to my statistic that I kept from the newspapers and you know the sources, the publishing sources. So, what happened? Why do bookshops, you know, keep closing down or has sold away the business? … Today, I'm going to explore on these topics.

 **2.05 Zhan**

Our DNA is our book of life. It contains three billion letters. That's three billion letters that define who we are. But, do you really know how that's done? Well, today I'm going to tell you how.

Technique	Dan	Zhan
Shocking statement or startling statistic	*It's around 35.*	*It contains three billion letters.*
Expert testimony or historical evidence	*That's according to my statistic that I kept from the newspapers and you know the sources, the publishing sources.*	
Enrolment questions	*So, I would like to start with a question. Do you know how many independent bookshops in Britain has closed in the last five months?*	
Question and answer	*So, what happened? Why do bookshops keep closing down? … Today, I'm going to explore on these topics.*	*But, do you really know how that's done? Well, today I'm going to tell you how.*

The other three techniques used by Dan and Zhan were:

1 Building rapport with the audience: *That's a good number.*
2 Analogy: *Our DNA is our book of life.*
3 Repetition: *It contains three billion letters. That's three billion letters.*

Note: Dan should have said:
Do you know how many independent bookshops in Britain have closed? (not *Do you know how many independent bookshop in Britain has closed?*)
I'm going to explore these topics. (not *I'm going to explore on these topics.*)

Grammar: Future continuous

A 1 'll be bringing   3 'll be examining
2 'll be looking   4 'll be outlining

B 1 'll be presenting   3 'd like
2 need   4 'll be showing

2 Finish with a bang
Introduction

A 1 A 'bang' can create anticipation and expectation, have an element of surprise, be dramatic, address the senses (visual, hearing), be humourous, involve the audience and be different. It should be given with power and conviction and be memorable. It must be relevant to the presentation and intensify the message.

B **2.06 Svitlana**

To summarise, I'll briefly take you through the main three points of my presentation with three proverbs. Firstly, learn the past of your country to avoid mistakes in the future. Secondly, you get what you fight for, so be ready. And thirdly, not everything that shines is gold which can be interpreted as 'be careful with what you're told by politicians' because the words and deeds are often different indeed.

1 Svitlana uses three Ukrainian familiar sayings or proverbs and links them to her summary. Such familiar sayings are also called aphorisms. The use of the technique is relevant. Svitlana's audience is the Oxford Ukrainian Society and there is every possibility that the audience will know the proverbs. They are relevant to the subject and final message. Nevertheless, the translation of the third proverb should be 'all that glitters is not gold'.
2 Her passion for the subject is obvious.

C **2.07 Zhan**

Let's just think about what we've talked about today. I've told you how DNA is translated into proteins, the building blocks of our lives. So, now, ladies and gentlemen, you know how our DNA, our book of life – our three billion letters – defines who we are.

1 Metaphor and analogy. The technique is relevant and the 'bang' was a mirror of his 'jump start'.
2 Yes, he said the same thing in three different ways (DNA, *our book of life, our three billion letters*).

Delivery: Verbal garbage

A **2.08 Dan**

Let's move on to the first, you know, slides. It's about the country. As you can see, it is the biggest country in the world, so, and the population is huge, which mean it's a huge market, it's a huge … it has potential to be, you know, to create a huge market there and … but if you look closely at the politics and the economic situation, we find that this country is not really stable, you know, comparing to other European countries. But I think with next slides, you will see that some more details in the book market itself which is appear quite different from what I just speak.
Now let's move on to the next slides. The first two, the first point I would like to make is the first two point here. Is the, you know the GDP per capita and the average salary monthly. Even though the number is not quite impressive, comparing to other European countries, I find that it's a very good market. If you look at the other two points, I like to point out it's the reading habits, and the Internet, you know, usings habit. I think this market, if you look from this point of view, this market is really mature … mature in terms of the, you know, if you want to put something new in because they got technologies, they've got, you know, they got love for the literature, the literacy level is very high comparing to, you know, their neighbour and also, you know, other countries

in the world. So I think it's really very good market in terms of that. And this is the, you know, the kind of economy in the … overview, so the next slides I will go into detail in a little bit into book market.

1 *You know*
2 It's very distracting. Sometimes, it's the only thing you hear and makes Dan's message difficult to understand.
3 Ten

B 🔘 2.09 **Dan**

Let's, let's turn to the first topics. The overall situation. What I would like to mention here is that there are two, two points that is the big, that is the situation that the small independent bookshops are facing now. The first one is the external one, and the other one is the internal one. Let's start with the internal one. Is the business itself is of the independent bookshop is I think what we can say is not … really efficient because it's quite a personal business, so that's why it can't compete to the multiple chains, or the, you know, the retailers, like as we all know in England is the WH Smith or those kind of thing, it can't compete. Why? Because … one is the stock, which is very important in the book market, because it's small bookshops can't compete, you know, with the keeping the stock of book, you know, compared to the bigger retailers, so that's the one problem, and the external one is that the business itself, you know, is very fierce. The competition is high because of the … the multiple retailers who, who have more power to negotiate of the price of the book or the publishers who still, you know, keep coming up with abusive discount rate. That's again, forced by the market itself. So, it's amazing how this, you know, some of the bookshops, the small bookshop is continuing to grow. But that happen too, you know so that's what I like to point out is that even though the many, many shops has closed, there are still more shops that open up in this … time so we'd like to explore on that a bit, but before I …

1 Seven
2 To a small extent he did, but he still needed to work on his verbal garbage. Even though Dan became conscious of his verbal garbage he could not eliminate it during the first practice after setting the target. Awareness is a first step in correcting errors and eliminating verbal garbage takes a lot of practice and repetition.

Delivery: Final consonant

D 🔘 2.10 **Svitlana**

Version 1

… that being nice to other people, showing tolerance, can help other people to improve.

Version 2

And to conclude, I would like to leave you with this thought: that being nice to other people, showing tolerance can really help some people to improve …

1 *tolerance*
2 *intolerance*
3 It completely changed part of her message.
4 She paused slightly between *showing* and *tolerance* and pronounced both words clearly.

3 **Full presentation**

🔘 2.11 **César**

Right. The protection of trademark law has been recently conceded to be the protection of the psychological functions of trademarks. In this presentation about trademark law I would like to give you an overview of what trademark law is about, why it's important, and how we protect trademarks in the market place. The points I will be addressing are, what is a trademark and how the concept of a trademark has evolved over the course of time. Why we think, and the law concedes, trademark law to be important, and trademarks in particular, why the protection is fundamental for the functioning and the smooth running of the market. And finally, I'll be looking at how, in the market place, trademarks are protected by courts and by the judges. So let me turn to my first point. 'What is a trademark?' is a question that all practitioners and all lawyers always ask themselves before turning to the question of infringement. Infringement is a point I will be addressing in the third point, now, I'll be coming to that later on. At this point, let me just say that a trademark is any sign that may function as an identifier of the origins of goods and as well as some sort of distinguisher that will tell the difference between some goods from other goods. That is the origin of some goods from one trader from another trader. To illustrate my point I would like to give you an example of Nike: as a word, Nike as a sign, and Nike as a slogan. All these three forms of a trademark are protected in different way and in different extent but they are all recognised by the law. So at this point I would like to say a few words about what is not a trademark and should not be confused with a concept of a trademark. The first one is a copyright. The second one is the concept of a patent, and the third one is the concept of a design. Each of these rights is independent in its own right and should be distinguished from the rest. The first one, copyright, is a right used to encourage art and literature and the production of books, and for this particular one we've got a different test which is that the work claiming to be protected should be original, it should have some creativity.

For a patent to be protected, we should be looking at whether or not the thing to be protected is or has been invented and is new. So at this point you can see that there is a big difference between saying 'I've got a copyright' or saying 'I've got a patent'. This is an invention, this is a creation. This is new, and this could be taken from already existing elements in nature. And the third one, which sometimes overlaps with the other rights is a design. A design could be something that is the outside appearance of a product, for example or a particular drawing, in the case of the fashion industry, for example. So, enough about the definition of a trademark and the difference between a trademark and other intellectual property rights.

Now let's move on to why we protect trademarks in the market place. At this point, I would like to draw your attention to the fact that trademark law is mainly concerned with the protection of consumers and the information that consumers get in the market place when they make purchasing decisions. Originally, and I'm talking about going back in time about a century ago, trademark law would always be concerned with the protection of the origin of the goods when they reached the consumer. Indirectly, trademark law also protected the traders that put the goods on the market, and the main protection was, if the consumer is not actually misled, right, then the trader should not be given an extra right. Over the past couple of years, protection has been moved from the main cornerstone, which is consumers, to traders, but that is a different point which I may be addressing in a minute. Now this brings me down to my third point, which is infringement. Just as the consumer has been the cornerstone of trademark protection, so has confusion, on the part of the consumer, has always been regarded as a cornerstone of protection. The question of whether or not the consumer is confused is relevant to whether or not you've got a right and you have a claim against another trader. However, the point of confusion, the element of confusion has been also expanded over the course of years, and now we've got different sorts of confusion. The more relevant, for example is origin confusion, and then affiliation confusion, and then sponsorship confusion. That's is not only the consumer thinks that the goods come from another manufacturer or the same manufacturer, but also if the consumer thinks that the manufacturer has endorsed… or another trader is affiliated with those goods on which the mark appears.

So, to summarise the three points I have made, let me just say that we've looked at the concept of a trademark and we've attempted to differentiate it from other intellectual property rights. Then we looked at why we are concerned with trademark law and on this point we looked at two main elements which are consumers and information. And finally on the question as to how we protect trademarks, we've looked at the main point, which is infringement and the cornerstone of infringement is confusion. So I hope that this overview of trademark law has given you a very important insight into the protection of trademarks and that might actually excite you and you might have found it a bit thought-provoking. Thank you very much for listening, and, please, if you have any questions, do ask. Thank you.

Step 3 Use visuals to connect
1 Visual aids
Interaction with visual aids: Number of slides

A 🔘 3.01 **Zhan**

Today, I'm going to talk to you about simulating genetic data. It is a very important aspect of what we do in mathematical genetics. It's currently not done very well. But today I'm going to introduce to you a new method developed by our group which is a significant improvement to the currently available methods of simulating genetic data. My name's Zhan Su. I'm a PhD student at the University of Oxford, and my presentation will be about five minutes, five to ten minutes and I'm happy to take any questions at the end.

So, first of all, this is what I'm going to talk to you about. I'm going to give you a brief overview of genetic data, what is it, why we want to simulate it and why is simulation so difficult. In the second part of my presentation, I will talk to you about the current methods of simulating genetic data, and there's two main methods that I'm going to talk about and they both have a problem and so in the final part of my talk, I'm going to talk, tell you about our method, which solves this problem, and I'm going to show you some results which demonstrate why it solves this problem.

So first of all we're going to talk about genetic data. OK, so what is genetic data? Our DNA consists of three billion letters A, T, C and Gs. But, at any particular site, a person can have at most two types. So that means we can condense this data, simplify this data, to a string of zero and ones. So now instead of talking about three billion letters, we are talking about three billion numbers and each one of those numbers is a zero or a one. So … genetic data in essence is a string of zero and ones.

So here is an example. Suppose we have two sets of genetic data. The first set are cases, so for example, those are genetic data of patients who have obesity, and the second set are control, so they're genetic data from people who does not have obesity, and mathematical geneticists will dream about a situation where you see something like this. So, as you can see, the cases all carry one type of a particular gene, the controls carry another type of this gene, so the gene coloured in red in essence could be a obesity-causing gene.

So, why would we want to simulate genetic data? Well, currently in the literature in my field, there is a lot of methods being published that claims to be better at locating disease genes. And the way you demonstrate why it is better is you apply it to a data set. You show that your predicted answer is very close to the actual real answer. However, there aren't that many data sets out there that you can apply it to, so think about it; if you know where the real answer is in these data sets, then you don't really need to develop new methods to detect them. So the way around this is you generate … simulated genetic data, you apply your method and you compare the real answer with the predicted answer. So that's why we want to simulate … genetic data.

But it's not always that simple, it's not just a case of generating random zeros and ones, because our genetic data is a product of thousands of generations, billions of years of evolution. So our genetic data is not random. There is a correlation structure in there that we need to simulate in our simulation haplotypes otherwise our data sets, our simulated data sets will be unrealistic. So … that's about what is genetic data, and why we want to simulate genetic data and why it's challenging to do so. Now we are going to look at some of the methods that are currently being done to simulate genetic data. So, there's two methods that I'm going to talk about. The first one is to simply simulate a group of individuals on the computer for, say, a thousand generations. You go through … so each generation, they pass on their genetic data to the next generation, there's mutation, there's kind of migration, there's selection, things going on. And after a thousand generations, you get your present day genetic data that you're looking for. This is quite tough, computationally because by simulating a thousand generations and thousands of individuals, that's going to take a lot of computing power.

The second method I'm going to talk about is … the second method that is quite popular at the moment is to essentially simulate it backwards in time using an approximation model called the coalescent. You don't really need to know too much about the coalescent model, you just need to think of it as an approximation through the evolution process. Both of these methods are quite widely used, but they both suffer from a common problem, and that is that you need to specify certain parameters beforehand, into their models. So these parameters are, for example, about population events. So the Black Plague wiped out about a third of the European population. That has a huge effect on the modern day genetic data that you see. So that sort of thing needs to be specified into these processes. There are other parameters such as mutation, selection, migration. All of these things need to be specified into the models, into the methods. The problem is, there is no definitive values, we don't really know what the right values for these parameters should be. We can give it a good guess, but if we guess wrong, our data sets that we simulate will be unrealistic. So this is not a very good situation at the moment.

So today, what I'm going to do, is to introduce to you a new method that we developed, that is, what we think, is much more realistic than the current … methods for simulating genetic data. And the way we are doing it is, so to look at real life, genetic data, those are available, and those have this correlation structure that we are trying to simulate. We are looking at real life genetic data, and we're looking at the structures there and we are using that to simulate … genetic data. So, we're going to use a Lee and Stevens Model. These two people introduced in 2003 a model for essentially genetic variation and what they're saying is that given you've seen K genetic, K chromosomes, you can generate a new chromosome by just taking a mosaic of the previously seen chromosomes. So let me just demonstrate what I mean. Here's how we generate our haplotypes to demonstrate what I mean. Suppose K equals four, so here are four chromosomes that we

see in real life, so this is realistic as you get. They contain the correlation structures that we are trying to copy. We can simulate our fifth genetic data by first looking at, just simulating at one site and then we are just copying from the previously seen … chromosome, so here we decide we are going to copy from number one, so there's a blue label, and we're going to progressively copy, from the first genetic data, from the first chromosome, but because of the mosaic at some point we're going to swap where we're going to copy from, so here, what we're going to do is we're going to decide, OK, we're going to copy from the third chromosome. There we go. And we can do the same on the left. So we're copying from the second chromosome and we keep on doing it, and there we go, there's our new chromosome that we've just simulated. And of course we do this stochastically so lots of different combinations are possible, so here's another combination that we could see, and we just carry on generating more and more genetic data this way.

So, I'm going to show you some results just to demonstrate why our methods is more realistic. For those of you who are familiar with recombination, at the bottom I've given you a graph that states recombination rates. If you don't know anything about recombination, ignore that. The top bit is a correlation matrix. Correlation matrix essentially visually encaptures the correlation structure in population data that we're trying to simulate. OK, you don't need to … if you don't really know anything about correlation matrices, don't worry about that, just remember that pattern. That pattern is what we are trying to recreate.

So here's the first simulated data that we see. At the bottom, if you're interested, is chi-square statistics. We've generated a disease gene where the blue line is. Don't worry too much about that if that confuses you. The main take-home message on this slide is to look at that correlation matrix. It is pretty much the same as the one we are trying to recreate. OK? So this is our simulated data, and we have simulated it realistically. Here's another simulated data set for those of you who are interested … at the bottom, we've increased the effect of the disease gene, so you get high chi-square statistics at the bottom. Don't worry about that if you don't understand that. The main thing is at the top we still see this correlation structure, so our data sets are realistic.

So that comes to the end of my presentation. Let's just think about what we've just gone through. What we said is, simulating genetic data is important, it's not done very well at the moment, but we have just introduced a model which does it better. How do we do it better? Well, we use real data. So, the very data we are trying to simulate, trying to copy, we use. We use the real data and we take into account the correlation structures that are present there to simulate new genetic data. And finally, our data is fast, so you can generate vast amounts of data. So in conclusion, what we've done is we've produced a new method, a new method that generates more realistic genetic data, and we believe this method will be very successful in the future. Thank you very much for listening, and now I'll take any questions you might have.

1 Seventeen (this excludes different versions of the same slide)

2 Seventeen slides in eleven minutes are probably too many. The audience's attention was drawn to the detailed information on the slides rather than to Zhan as the presenter.

3 **Suggestions**
Simulating Haplotypes – (just keep headlines and remove details)
What is genetic data?
Either Why do we simulate genetic data? or Why is simulating genetic data challenging?
Problems with current methods
Simulating from real genetic data
Summary
In any case, many of the slides need to be simplified so that the audience can take in the message. Such detailed information can be given be in a handout after the presentation.

B **Suggestions**

1 Probably reading.

2 Some presenters think that if they put enough detail on slides, they can read and this will help their English. They achieve exactly the opposite effect.

3 Too much detailed information means that the audience begins to read rather than listen to the presentation.

4 No. This was a critical point of the presentation and the audience's attention should have been fully on Zhan. It would have been better to cut the slide completely.

5 No.

Interaction with visual aids: Bullet point lists

C **Suggestions**

What is genetic data?
- string of 4 letters, e.g. …AGGGGATTTAAA…
- 1 or 2 types → …0101001010101…

Why do we simulate genetic data?
- many methods
- assessment
- requirements
- conclusion

Why is simulating genetic data challenging?
- real genetic data
- complex structures
- simulated data

Interaction with visual aids: Procedure

D 3.02 **Zhan**

So, I'm going to show some results just to demonstrate why our methods is more realistic. For those of you who are familiar with recombination, at the bottom I've given you a graph that states the recombination rates. If you don't know anything about recombination, ignore that. The top bit is a correlation matrix. Correlation matrix essentially visually encaptures the correlation structure in population data that we're trying to simulate. OK, you don't need to … if you don't really know anything about correlation matrices, don't worry about that, just remember that pattern. That pattern is what we're trying to recreate.
So, here's the first simulated data that we see. At the bottom, if you're interested, is chi-square statistics. We've generated a disease gene where the blue line is. Don't worry too much about that if that confuses you. The main take-home message on this slide is to look at that correlation matrix. It is pretty much the same as the one we are trying to recreate. OK. So, this is our simulated data and we have simulated it realistically. Here's another simulated data set for those of you who are interested … at the bottom, we've increased the effects of the disease gene, so you get high chi-squared statistics at the bottom. Don't worry about that if you don't understand that – the main thing is at the top we still see this correlation structure, so our data sets are realistic.

E 1 He draws audience's attention to the diagram.

2 He explains the matrix in general terms so that the audience can become familiar with it and understand it.

3 He says what the most important part is.

4 He gives the message or conclusion.

F 1 I'd like us to focus our attention on … 1

2 What is interesting / important here is … 3

3 I'm sure the implications are clear to all of us … 4

4 The figures in this table show … 2

5 It is important to notice that … 3

6 The take-home message here is …4

7 We can conclude that … 4

8 This chart compares … 2

9 I'd like you to think about … 3

10 If you look at the top right hand corner … 2

11 The lesson we can learn from this is … 4

12 The blue dotted line represents … 2

13 The top half shows … 2

14 Now, I'll show you … 1

15 Let's move on now and look at the figures for … 1

16 The significance of this is … 4

17 I would like you to concentrate on this green column … 3

18 The next overhead shows … **1**

19 As we can see … **3** or **4**

20 The vertical axis represents … **2**

Interaction with visual aids: Take a risk!

G 3.03 **Zhan**

So, that comes to the end of my presentation. Let's just think about what we've just gone through. What we said is, simulating genetic data is important, it's not done very well at the moment, but we have just introduced a model which does it better. How do we do it better? Well, we use real data. So, the very data we're trying to simulate, trying to copy, we use. We use the real data and we take into account the correlation structures that are present there to simulate new genetic data. And finally, our data is fast, so you can generate vast amounts of data. So, in conclusion, what we've done is we've produced a new method, a new method that generates more realistic genetic data and we believe that this method will be very successful in the future. Thank you very much for listening, and now I will take any questions you might have.

1 There is probably too much information on the summary chart. It would have been better to have used key words or even no chart at all as the audience attention was drawn to reading the chart and not listening to Zhan's take home message.

2 So, in conclusion what we've done is we've produced a new method, a new method that generates more realistic genetic data and we believe that this method will be very successful in the future.

3 Zhan wanted to 'sell' his new method and although his conclusion is verbally clear, both his and his audience's attention were directed to the summary chart. There was therefore confusion in the take-home message and the final message lost impact and 'bang'.

H 3.04 **Svitlana**

That brings me to end of my presentation.

To summarise, I'll run through three main points again. First, get prepared before the trip. Second, follow the rules. Third, take care while getting around.

This leads me to a conclusion that as long as you use common sense and look after each other, you should be absolutely fine and will enjoy your visit to this magnificent destination. And to finish on a bright note, please look at me. Do you like my outfit? Do you like my shoes? These shoes are sold in the UK for £20. You can buy them in India for £2. The shopping is excellent in India and it is another thing to look forward to.

Thank you very much for your time and if you have any questions, I will be very happy to answer them now.

1 Svitlana used her shoes and clothes as visual aids.

2 The answer here is subjective and to some extent depends on personal style and the type of business you are involved in. Sometimes though; it is worth considering taking a risk to add impact and 'bang'.

2 Numbers and trends

Numbers and approximations

A 1 four thousand five hundred and seventy-nine employees

2 thirty point three, three metres

3 nine hundred and ninety-five dollars

4 seven point three, eight, five percent

5 five point one million euros

B 1 around four thousand five hundred employees

2 just over thirty metres

3 one thousand dollars more or less

4 approximately seven point four per cent

5 roughly five million euros

C **Suggestions**

1 We have nearly 700 offices in just over 150 cities worldwide.

2 Our revenue was well over €300 billion last year.

3 There was more than a 5.5% increase in sales.

4 The ingredients are round about 80% water.

5 Just under 80% stated a strong preference for Product Y.

6 In Europe the category spending has been just under $13 million and has been down by less than 0.5% in the last twelve months.

7 The total forecast value is roughly £2,700.

8 Australia has over 190,000 professional engineers.

9 It's a fast process – less than 30 seconds.

10 We manufacture well above 700 products.

Trends

B bottom out, climb, come down, decrease, deteriorate, deterioration, double, drop, even out, fall, fluctuate, fluctuation, go down, go up, grow, growth, hit a low, hold firm, improve, improvement, increase, jump, level off, peak, pick up, plunge, reach a peak, recover, recovery, remain stable, remain steady, rocket, shoot up, shrink, slump, stabilise, stagnate, stagnation, slip back, take off, ups and downs.

C 1 1 took off   3 recover
    2 slumped   4 improvement

2 1 slipped back   4 doubled
    2 plunged   5 remained stable
    3 rocketed

3 1 ups and downs 3 holding firm
  2 fluctuated 4 stabilise

4 1 gone up 3 shot up
  2 jump

Grammar: Adjectives and adverbs

B considerable, considerably, dramatic, dramatically, gradual, gradually, rapid, rapidly, sharp, sharply, significant, significantly, slight, slightly, steady, steadily, substantial, substantially, sudden, suddenly.

C 1 dramatically 5 gradual
  2 steadily 6 rapid
  3 slight 7 sharp
  4 considerably 8 slightly

Grammar: Prepositions

D 1 by 6 by
  2 to 7 to
  3 from 8 of
  4 to 9 in
  5 between 10 at

E 1 1 climbed
    2 has rocketed
    3 will go up

  2 1 rose 5 has been
    2 remained 6 is levelling off
    3 reached 7 will hit
    4 had been falling

F **Suggestions**
  1 Sales climbed gradually last June.
    Past simple – trend that happened in the past and is finished.
  2 They had increased slightly before the joint venture.
    Past perfect – a trend that had already happened when we talk about the past.
  3 They grew steadily last November.
    Past simple – trend that happened in the past and is finished.
  4 They have shot up from last November to now.
    Present perfect – a trend that started in the past and isn't finished.
  5 Now sales are rocketing.
    Present continuous – a trend that is happening now.
  6 They'll decline rapidly next January.
    will in predictions of future trends.

G **Suggestions**
  1 We expect business to pick up next year.
  2 I anticipate a downturn.
  3 I forecast an increase in sales.
  4 We foresee a dramatic change in the market.
  5 I predict it won't sell.

3 Full presentation

3.05 César

Good morning everyone. Feel very welcome to my presentation. Let me just introduce myself. My name is César Ramirez, and I am a trademark solicitor, and this morning, I am going to give you an overview of what I do, and I have chosen a particular topic and that's called 'trade dress'. So, it tastes like, it smells like and it looks like, but it's not the same thing. I'll be addressing three main points in my presentation. The first one will be what I mean by 'trade dress', what the subject matter is, and the definition of that and I'll give you several examples along the course. And in my second point I would like to talk about the different actions that we may take to stop trade dress infringement. And finally in my third point, I'll be looking at why we actually protect trade dress and why it's actually important, and relevant to the public.

So, moving on to my first point, the subject matter, what trade dress is. Trade dress briefly is the general appearance, or the visual appearance of a particular product. So to illustrate my point, I will be looking at three different examples of trade dress. The first one will be the configuration of a product, the second one will be the shape of the product and the third one will be the design of the product.

So, moving on to my first example: the configuration of a product. Here, we've got two different products, right, two tins of Coke. So, this is, as you all know, this is a tin of Coke, right, and next to it we've got its twin, right, and what I mean by 'trade dress' is basically the copying or imitation of certain characteristics of an original product and used on a different product, to actually make it look like the same product. In this case, for example, we've got the colour, right, which is red, the graphics, the script is very similar – Coke to Cola – and also the use of commonplace words, in this case Cola, Coke, Coca Cola and Cola or Classic Cola. Cola is a generic word which can be used by all traders.

Moving on to my second example, this concerns the shape of the product. In this case we've got some Head and Shoulders shampoo. In this case, right, the shape of the product, the general appearance of the product has been copied. There was no reason for it, because they could have chosen a completely different shape of the bottle. Nevertheless, the shape was copied, and also certain elements of the visual appearance and the size of it were copied. As you can see for example, Head and Shoulders is very similar to Headway, right and this combination of colours was also sort of copied on the fake product.

Moving on to my third point: the design of a product. In this case, for example, Corn Flakes made by Kellogg's uses a very particular – well, it's not very particular because it's mainly used by most cereals, right, nevertheless the sort of graphic configuration, the arrangement of the colours, and certain patterns within the design of Corn Flakes were copied and at the same time or by doing that, the new product, the new entrant is actually transferring some of the imagery or some of the commercial attractions, some of the commercial magnetism of the first product, the famous product onto the new product. So at this point I have actually looked at three different ways or three different products, that have been copied and imitated in three different forms. The first one was the configuration, then the shape and then the design of a product.

So enough about the subject matter, let's move on to my next point which is the infringement action. And so, in this regard let me just say that in order to tackle these three problems, a trademark practitioner would normally use three different sorts of action. The first one is the traditional likelihood of confusion. The second one is a traditional, not traditional, sorry, the new form of dilution, and the third one is unfair competition. The first one I've mentioned, confusion, is normally a bit, rather limited, because it does not cover instances where … to prove confusion, consumer confusion would be very difficult. As you can see the names are different, so a case for confusion would be very difficult to prove because the name of the product, the name of the brand is not actually used. It's very intelligent, they actually used just the configuration but not the name. And as you can see the name of the new product is actually predominantly displayed. So instances of confusion will be dispelled. The second action, which is dilution is a more complicated one, but suffice to say at this point that it is normally used when there is some damage – not to the public … in the form of confusion but its damage to the mark itself, to the brand itself. When the general commercial magnetism of the brand will be diminished or will be damaged by the use of a similar or identical trade dress on a competitor's product, on a similar product or an identical product. And a third action which I believe is the best and most effective way to tackle this problem is unfair competition and unfair competition will provide us with a remedy if we can prove that the elements that are being copied – let me just go back a bit – if the elements that are being copied are not functional or generic, then we may have an action. In this case for example we could argue that this is functional and it just makes it easier to handle the bottle of shampoo. And possibly, you may also argue that the shape of a tin of Coke is actually functional and generic, because it makes it easier to drink a tin of Coke like that as opposed to, you know, having a different shape. So if we can prove that the elements we are actually claiming protection on are not functional then we may have redress through an action of unfair competition.

So, moving on to my last point, let me just say a few words about why we're interested in protecting trade dress and at this point there are three main interests. The first one is the

investment of the trader, in this case the owner of Coca Cola, the Kellogg's company and the owner of the Head and Shoulders company. They invest in not only advertising, but developing other products, and they are obviously interested in preserving this commercial magnetism which they actually develop through advertising. The second interest which I believe is the most important one, the keystone, is the public interest, and this is concerned with the protection of consumers – that the consumers should not be confused with buying a similar product. When you go to Sainsbury's, for example, say, if you are in a rush, you haven't got time to actually check the product, you may actually grab Sainsbury's Coke as opposed to Coca Cola. So the interest there is to protect the consumer.

And the last interest is fair practices. That one trader should not actually free-ride or gain an advantage over another without actually spending money, time and effort.

So to summarise what we've looked at: we've looked at the definition of a trade dress, and to illustrate my definition, I gave you three different examples. And the second point we looked at was the three different actions we can actually invoke to get protection, and the third one was the different interests at stake when protecting trade dress. I trust that you have got a very clear insight into what I do regarding trademark infringement actions, in particular trade dress. I am very happy to take any questions, and to thank you very much for listening.

Step 4 Top up your techniques

1 Powerful Techniques
Introduction

C So, what is our second graduate programme? [**rhetorical question**]

This is our high potential Summit programme that will take the best among you to the top, the very top. [**mantra**]

This is a very exciting option for those of you who are truly looking for variety, opportunity and challenge. [**rule of three**]

The programme enables you to take on three different assignments in three countries in three years [**rule of three**] and at the same time study for postgraduate management and language qualifications.

It's a challenge, a real challenge. [**repetition**]

Your first assignment takes place in your home country, the second at our headquarters in San Diego and the third in another country where we expect you to learn a new language. [**rule of three**]

Of course, we pay for all your relocation and study expenses. In fact, our support is very generous, very generous, [**repetition**] indeed more generous than [**contrast**] anything else you'll find on the job market.

But, in return you have to be flexible, hard-working and

self-motivated [**rule of three**] because this programme is not a holiday but a boot camp. [**contrast**]

You will work, work, work and study, study, study. [**rule of three**]

We test you and you test us. If you successfully finish the three assignments, you are not simply at the end of your training but at the beginning [**contrast**] of a fast, interesting and rewarding [**rule of three**] career path on your way to the top, the very top. [**mantra**]

Let me give you an example of [**example**] a Summit success story. This is Milena Gawczynski. She had the best degree of her year from Warsaw University and a MBA that she completed during her year with us in San Diego. Her third year on the Summit programme was spent in Barcelona where she initiated a project to improve communications between our southern European manufacturing plants. She speaks fluent Polish, Russian, English and Spanish and is currently head of our Central European Services office in Prague.

As you can see, our standards are much higher than [**contrast**] other companies. Our assessment centre is far more rigorous than [**contrast**] all the others presented to you today. That's because we only want the best and of course you'll get the best [**repetition**] from us. Our 'summiteers' earn above average salaries and performance bonuses. Our mentoring scheme, international networks and development programme [**rule of three**] are second to none. If it's variety, opportunity and challenge [**rule of three and repetition**] you're looking for and you know you are the best, then, our Summit programme is the one for you. It's the only one that will take you to the top, the very top. [**mantra**]

Repetition, repetition

B 4.01 Svitlana

1 *You'll drive back home or wherever you're going afterwards **carefully**, very **carefully**, even if you are late you will drive **carefully**.*

2 ***Who, who** makes it dangerous? **You, you** my dear people, car drivers, taxi drivers and bus drivers. **You, you** my dear people make life of cyclists every day's challenge.*

3 *Remember **however in a hurry** you are, **however in a hurry** your passengers are, there are definitely many more important things to life than being on time.*

4 *Which means that you've got a **much, much** better chance to knock down a cyclist.*

5 ***They do not give you the right** of not being careful. **They do not give you the right** to overtake cyclists sharply. **They do not give you the right** to break the speed limits even when the roads look empty.*

6 ***Big bus, big bus, big** danger.*

4.01 César

1 *Intellectual property is undeniably present in **every single part** of our lives, **every single part**.*

2 ***Whatever** we do, wherever we are, **whatever** we see, **whatever** we hear is all related to intellectual property.*

3 *So the current situation really makes us wonder whether the countries that **so ferociously** promote intellectual property and **so ferociously** want to have their own creations protected, are actually consistent with the way intellectual property originated.*

4 *Back then intellectual property protection was **literally** non-existent compared to our 21st century, for example, where IP laws are **literally, literally** omnipresent.*

5 *I cannot really see any reason why we should continue to perpetuate by giving **loads** and **loads** of protection to some and increasing the losses of others.*

6 *Intellectual property rights last for a **very, very** long time.*

7 *The drive for monopoly is **very, very** strong.*

Repeated words are highlighted in bold.

Mantra

A 4.02 Svitlana

1 *Cycling is fast, convenient, non-polluting way to get around.*

2 *Let's agree that cycling is fast, convenient, and non-polluting.*

3 *Driving is obviously fast when you don't get stuck in traffic, convenient, but polluting way to get around.*

4 *Buses are fast, convenient (when you don't get squashed between two sweaty bodies in the rush hour!), but again polluting way to get around.*

5 *Cycling is fast, convenient and non-polluting way to get around.*

1 fast, convenient, (non-)polluting

2 It would have been more dramatic to build up to the change 'non-polluting' and to have had this as the last point rather than as the first point. Svitlana also breaks the mantra up by using different words in the middle of the mantra. So, it is not really 'to the point' and it loses effect. However, using mantra is not easy and experimenting with the technique is the first step to improvement.

Rhetorical questions

A Suggestions

1 How many people do we employ?

2 How many did we hire in the Netherlands?

3 What are we doing?

4 When are we going to start?

5 Is there a solution?

6 Have we ever used an external company?

7 What do I recommend?

8 What's the next step?

9 What's my second point?

10 What's the answer?

B Suggestions

1 How did we do this?

2 How should we do this?

3 Can we improve even more next year?

4 How are we going to do this?

5 So, what's my third point?

6 Where have we been most successful?

7 What were the reasons for this?

8 Why does it happen again and again?

9 Why?

10 Why did the client hate what we loved?

C

a What does this mean?

b What did we do? or What have we done?

c How often do you speak English in meetings?

d Does the client accept our changes?

e Did we make the changes?

f What are we doing about this?

Delivery: Intonation in questions

D 4.03 César

Is not a lifetime enough to recoup what you have invested in?

Do we really need to give them another 100 years?

Are we not actually going too far?

Rule of Three

A Suggestions

Friends, Romans, Countrymen (William Shakespeare in Julius Caesar)

Blood, sweat and tears (General Patton)

Our priorities are Education, Education, Education (Tony Blair)

Life, liberty, and the pursuit of happiness (the American Declaration of Independence)

Government of the people, by the people, for the people (the Gettysburg Address)

There are three kinds of lies: lies, damned lies, and statistics (Benjamin Disraeli)

This is not the end. It is not even the beginning of the end. But it is, perhaps, the end of the beginning (Sir Winston Churchill)

Happiness is when what you think, what you say, and what you do are in harmony (Mahatma Gandhi)

location, location, location

tall, dark and handsome

up, up and away

ready, steady, go

work harder, faster, smarter

Father, Son and Holy Ghost

Faith, Hope and Charity

Today, Tomorrow, Toyota

Speed, ease, value – Euro tunnel

B 4.04 Svitlana

Let's start then. Let's look at cycling first. Cycling is fast, convenient and non-polluting way to get around.

You, you my dear people make life of cyclists every day's challenge, every day's fight for life, every day's struggle.

And that means that you need to be even more careful. I know, I know, I know that you have to follow a tight schedule, that your passengers might get annoyed if you don't overtake a slow cyclist, that you are sick and tired of cyclists jumping the red light …

The only recommendation I can make and I insist on you following it is: drive carefully, drive carefully, drive carefully.

1 fast, convenient and non-polluting way to get around.

2 challenge / fight for life / struggle

3 know, I know, I know

4 have to follow / might get annoyed / sick and tired

5 drive carefully, drive carefully, drive carefully

Examples

A 4.05 César

So let me take you back to the seventeenth, eighteenth and nineteenth century. Back then, intellectual property protection was literally non-existent compared to our twenty-first century, for example, where IP laws are literally, literally omnipresent.

So, back then we had no intellectual property protection, so we had no copyright protection, no patents and no trademark rights.

My question to you is, 'Would or would not Michelangelo have produced the quality of works that he made, the quality of the sculptures that he sculpted and the quality of paintings that he painted because of a lack of intellectual property protection?'

Most of us would answer certainly by saying 'no'.

1 Michelangelo

2 Yes, everyone knows the example.

3 Yes, it makes the audience imagine a world without the works of Michelangelo. It adds power and weight to César's argument about intellectual property protection.

Contrast: Grammar: Comparisons

A
1 better	3 worse	
2 more appealing	4 bigger	

B
1 a little	3 roughly	
2 much	4 just	

C 1 considerably / much 3 almost / nearly
    2 slightly / a little 4 virtually / roughly

Contrast: Opposites

D 1 light 8 cold 15 failure
    2 weak 9 finish 16 allow
    3 wrong 10 down 17 new / young
    4 slow 11 short 18 hate
    5 after 12 take 19 late
    6 lie 13 night 20 bottom
    7 die 14 bad

Not X but Y

E  4.06 Svitlana

1 *I don't argue the fact that you might have a very good reason to pollute … but when your kids grow up, …*

2 *You have to not only obey the road rules, but take care of the people on the road.*

3 *Because you are responsible not only for your life, but for [the] lives of your passengers as well.*

Advanced signposting

A 1 c 2 e 3 f 4 b 5 g 6 a 7 d

2 Full presentation

4.07 César

Hello everyone. Good afternoon. Very welcome to my presentation on IP trends and let me introduce myself. My name is César Ramirez, and today I would like to give you an overview of intellectual property trend, and my main purpose today is actually to ask questions and possibly to raise some doubts as to where intellectual property is going and where it should go. So the first point I will be addressing will be the ubiquity of intellectual property, and then my second point will be the omnipresence of intellectual property, and finally the third point I'll be looking at is the over-protection of intellectual property.

In the old days, a glimpse of stocking was thought of as shocking. But now, heaven knows, anything goes. So this rhetoric actually I believe, applies to current trends of intellectual property.

So, let me start off, by discussing my first point, the ubiquity of intellectual property. Intellectual property is undeniably present in every single part of our lives – every single part of our lives. And by this I mean that whatever we do, wherever we are, whatever we see, whatever we hear is all related to intellectual property. At home, we've got computers, we've got Internet connection, we eat packaged goods, we wear certain clothes, we drive certain cars. Each of these cars may have patented parts, or maybe a trademark, or maybe a copyright design, for example. When you go to work, you've got colleagues, and your colleagues write emails, they write pieces of paper, they give presentations, they

write books, etc. And all these creative works are all protected by intellectual property. So the point I'm trying to make here, is how ubiquitous intellectual property is in our lives. In other words, how pervasive it has become.

Moving on to my second point is the omnipresence of intellectual property. It is true that intellectual property is very different, intellectual property today I mean is very different to intellectual property laws in the nineteenth century. Nowadays a country that does not afford intellectual property protection is regarded as a country that promotes piracy, and is very likely to be put on a black list by intellectual property organisations. But let me take you back to the nineteenth century – specifically to the eighteenth century and the nineteenth century. Let me take you back to the US. In most of the nineteenth century, the US did not grant any copyright protection to foreigners. The main purpose or the main policy of the country was to disseminate and to promote culture and knowledge by using British works. Charles Dickens, for example, was ridiculed when he toured the country promoting intellectual property rights for authors and writers. Nowadays any country not complying with intellectual property regimes will be automatically black-listed and shunned by the United States. The same would be done by European countries. So the current situation really makes us wonder whether the countries that so ferociously promote intellectual property, and so ferociously want to have their own creations protected are actually consistent with the way intellectual property originated, and if their discourse is actually consistent with what they used to actually do in the past. Let me just further expand on this point. Let me pose some questions to you. So, let me take you back to the seventeenth, eighteenth and nineteenth century. Back then, intellectual property protection was literally non-existent compared to our twenty-first century, for example, where IP laws are literally, literally omnipresent. So, back then we had no intellectual property protection, so we had no copyright protection, no patents and no trademark rights. My question to you is, 'Would, or would not Michelangelo have produced the quality of works that he made, the quality of the sculptures that he sculpted and the quality of paintings that he painted because of a lack of intellectual property protection?' Most of us would answer certainly by saying 'no'. And so let me also ask you this question about the eighteenth century when intellectual property was not even recognised by the US, 'Would Charles Dickens have produced less works and have written less novels, and less quality of stories because of a lack of intellectual property?' The answer again is certainly 'no'.

So despite the absence of intellectual property protection, there was an encouragement and there was a desire to produce, to write and to disseminate the works of the mind, so given the general status quo of intellectual property at the moment, I cannot really see any reason why we should continue to perpetuate by giving loads and loads of protection to some and increasing the losses of others. In other words, the more protection we give them, the less impoverished we become.

So let me move on to my third point about the over protection of intellectual property and at this point let me just emphasise that intellectual property rights last for a very, very long time. Take for example copyright. At the moment copyright protection lasts for the life of the author plus, on average, fifty years. The US and the European Union recognise seventy years, while other countries recognise a hundred years. So my question to you is, 'Are we really encouraging, or is it really desirable for society to maintain a monopoly on a particular work of the mind for such a long time, when one of the objectives and main purposes of intellectual property is to encourage creativity and at the same time to give creators and writers just enough to recoup the investment that they have made into their creations?' Is not a lifetime enough to recoup what you have invested in? Do we really need to give them another hundred years? Are we not actually going too far? Now, if I take patents for example, originally patent law was specifically designed to promote and encourage inventions by granting protection to those creators and inventors that produced creations if they meet certain criteria. The criteria was novelty, non-obviousness and industrial application. Nowadays patent law will protect not only a business method, but also DNA and gene sequences. The question that this movement in the law arises is, 'Do we really consider a business method absolutely new?' Have we not actually, or do we not actually take and copy what others do on an everyday basis? Are these people actually creating something out of the new that did not exist in nature? Do they really deserve to gain a monopoly over something that they might have actually copied from someone else?

So this last point brings me to … the conclusion of my presentation. And to summarise the points I have discussed: we've looked at the ubiquity of intellectual property. We saw how pervasive intellectual property is in our everyday lives. We've seen how intellectual property is omnipresent nowadays and we've also looked at how intellectual property has gone a bit too far by over-protecting certain creations and certain inventions. Now just to leave you with a bit of a thought-provoking statement, I would like to say to you this: In a modern society, the drive for monopoly is very, very strong. Unchecked, I am very certain that this drive would copyright the alphabet, patent the wheel and trademark the sun. Lest we forget, intellectual property is for the benefit of us, not for our impoverishment. Thank you very much for listening, and I am very happy to take any questions you may have.

Step 5 Be positive and dramatic

1 Be positive

Power words: The Yale 12

A The words are powerful because they affect us directly and everyone is concerned with health, safety, relationships and security.

B

1	You	5	easy	9	health
2	love	6	results	10	guarantee
3	new	7	proven	11	save
4	discover	8	safety	12	money

Power words: Common power words

C The following are often added as a secondary list to the Yale 12.

free	now	what
imagine	I wonder if	why
most	success	who
greatest	best	how
announcing	now	how to

The following can also be considered power words and phrases:

powerful	secret	revealed
you'll love this	the best kept secret	scientific
hottest	unbelievable	shocked
improved	breakthrough	shocking
revolutionary	hidden	ultimate
state-of-the-art	incredible	uncovered
fantastic	master	your
for a limited time only	profits	

Grammar: Conditional sentences

A 1 We would lose credibility and market share if we decided to stay here.
   If we moved to another location, our corporate identity would suffer greatly.
   If we build our own offices, we will strengthen our image, improve internal communications and provide room for further expansion and success whilst maintaining our basic structure and values.

   2 The presenter uses the 2nd conditional to present the options he / she sees as hypothetical and doesn't want the audience to accept, and the 1st conditional for the option he / she sees as the possible outcome he / she wants the audience to accept. He / She builds a strong recommendation by presenting hypothetical options first and presenting the possible recommendation last.

B Suggestions

   1 If we decided to go in this direction, there would be a number of problems.
   2 If we wanted to do this, the client would have a number of questions.
   3 If we take this option, we'll have a better long-term solution.
   4 If you made a decision to go with XYZ, our company would not be the one for you.

5 If you buy this product, you'll have the best product for the job.

6 If you continued in this way, you would experience a complete breakdown in the system.

7 If you employed an external company, the costs would be enormous.

8 If you simply restructure, you will save both time and money.

Convincing language

A **Proposal A**

Let me then turn to the third and final option which is to move to new offices near the airport. There **are** some drawbacks to this option as the process of finding a location, building to our specifications and moving **will** be costly and time-consuming. We **shouldn't** worry too much about these drawbacks though as the advantages outweigh the disadvantages. I **suggest** that we find a location where we can build to our specifications in a way that reflects our corporate image. Clients **could** get to our offices more easily from the airport and we **should** be able to build an underground garage so that there**'ll** be more visitor parking. In addition, you **find** good accommodation around the airport. **Hopefully**, we **could** restructure the offices so that we **maybe** can improve internal communication and leave room for new departments as we **perhaps** grow. We **should** stick to our corporate values and **many** of our staff will **probably** stay with us.

Proposal B

Let me then turn to the third, final and **best** option which is to move to new offices near the airport. There could be some **minor** drawbacks to this option as the process of finding a location, building to our specifications and moving **might** be costly and time-consuming. We should **not** worry about these drawbacks though as the advantages **far** outweigh the disadvantages. I **strongly recommend** that we find a location where we can build to our specifications in a way that reflects our corporate image. Clients **will** get to our offices more easily from the airport and we **are going to** build an underground garage so that there will be more visitor parking. In addition, you **do** find good accommodation around the airport. What **we'll do is** restructure the offices so that we**'ll certainly** improve internal communication and leave room for new departments as we grow. We **plan** to stick to our corporate values and to **keep most** of our staff.

B **Suggestions**

1 I trust you understood my message.
2 It will definitely be successful.
3 We believe we can do that for you.

4 This is a very interesting idea.
5 We should certainly go in that direction.
6 I strongly recommend you go with this campaign.
7 These findings indicate we must do this.
8 We're positive that it is right.

D 1 I think it is time for a change.
2 We do not believe this is a good idea.
3 The candidate did not meet our requirements.
4 He did meet all our requirements.
5 She is going to write a new specification.
6 This is not an option I recommend.
7 The research does show that we do have to modify the product.
8 What they are proposing is not feasible.

Delivery: Pronunciation

A Incorrectly pronounced keywords: *process, gases, surface, carbon dioxide, methane, ozone, 1715*

2 Be dramatic

Techniques: Metaphor and analogy

B 🔘 **5.02 Zhan**

Let me just digress for a second. Some of you might have seen these films. The Matrix, Terminator or iRobot and all these films tell a story of humans against machines. After seeing these films you might also get the idea that actually humans are not that different from machines. Whereas machines are made of inorganic materials such as metals, our bodies are made of organic materials such as proteins. Whereas machines are designed from a blueprint, our bodies are designed from blueprint encoded in our DNA. And, finally, whereas machines break down, our bodies succumb to disease. In essence our bodies are machines. And I would just like to go back to that third point I mentioned which is machines breaking down. Machines break down because they haven't been maintained properly and likewise our bodies break down because we haven't been taking care of it properly. We're talking about, for example, bad diet, lack of exercise or a bad environment. But machines also break down because it hasn't been designed properly. There may be a design fault and likewise there are design faults in our DNA. There are errors in our DNA which causes disease. So, those are genetic diseases and here is a list of some of those that you might have heard of.

Suggestions

1 Zhan compares human bodies to machines, using references to three well-known films. He extends the analogy by comparing the make-up of machines and bodies and the blueprints for design bringing in the link to DNA. Finally, he compares design faults in machines

and bodies, pointing out that errors in DNA lead to genetic disease.

2 This is subjective and forming your opinion is part of the process of finding your voice. However, Zhan's audience considered it an excellent analogy – especially for non-specialists. He makes his points clearly and simply. There is a clear link between the analogy and the presentation message.

G ⏺ 5.03 Svitlana

I will tell you the elephant story. If you have ever been to a circus or zoo, you have probably wondered why it is that the huge, old elephants and tiny baby elephants tethered with exactly the same chain. A fully grown-up elephant could, if it wanted to, simply walk away without even breaking into a sweat. But, that's just the point. The old elephant has forgotten what it is like to struggle, to be free. The baby elephant, who constantly pulls and tugs at its chain, still has the motivation to succeed. That's the end of the story. **So, let's be the baby elephants and struggle for the better environment.**

2 circus, tethered, sweat

3 See bold in transcript.

4 Yes, she Keeps It Short and Simple and makes a link in one quick sentence. She repeats vocabulary from the story in her presentation message.

Techniques: Anecdote

I ⏺ 5.04 Zhan

I've highlighted obesity because that's quite topical at the moment.. And this was an article in a Times earlier this month, and what this article is about, is that scientists found a obesity gene. So, which means that patients who carry this gene are more likely to have obesity, irrespective of their diet, of their environment or of their exercise habits. So, that's essentially what we do …

… And just to finish off. This is a Times article which was actually front page news last week and what this story says is that pharmaceutical companies hope to be able to make a pill that negates the effects of faulty genes, of disease genes. So, this is for the first time this is kind of evidence that offers us hope of a real cure, an actual cure for genetic diseases.

1 Zhan used two up-to-date articles. The first described how scientists discovered an obesity gene and the second described how pharmaceutical companies hope to make drugs to cure genetic disease.

2 The first article made a link from Zhan's point about errors in DNA and genetic disease and gave a clear example of this. The second demonstrated the overall aims for Zhan's research.

3 Zhan used current articles and showed an awareness of the world around him. The audience were probably

aware of the articles too and it made the presentation very relevant to their needs and concerns.

4 Zhan could have taken a lot of the text out of the articles and used the pictures and headlines in the presentation. An obesity picture tells a thousand words, for example, and has a dramatic impact. The full texts could have been given as a handout.

Techniques: Self disclosure

J 1 You learn something about the presenter outside of her business life.

2 The presenter tells a story about a personal failure and shows a human side. The audience engage with her as they become involved in the story. As they become involved, they empathise.

3 Different presentation messages could evolve from this story, e.g. you need to fail in order to succeed, firing staff for one mistake is not the answer, learn to focus totally on your goal.

K ⏺ 5.05 Zhan

Step 1

Morning everyone. I'm Zhan Su. I'm a statistics department PhD student at the University of Oxford, and today I'm going to tell you a little bit about my research. I'm going to briefly tell you what I do, briefly tell you how I do it and finally I'm going to tell you why I do it. The presentation should last about five minutes, and I'm happy to take any questions after that.

So first of all, what is it I do? So, I work in a field called mathematical genetics, and essentially what we do is try to locate those part of our genome, those part of our DNA, that causes disease. So if you imagine our bodies to be machines, then like any other machine, our bodies are prone to break down. So some of that is because we haven't been taking care of it very well, so for example, bad diet, lack of exercise. But some of the reasons are because our bodies is not built very well, and the reason why that is, is because there are faults in our DNA. Our DNA are the blueprints to our bodies, to the machines. So what we do is try to locate those parts of our DNA that causes these diseases. So I've just listed some of those diseases that you might recognise. This whole topic is quite topical, quite relevant at the moment because a couple of days ago, there was an article in the BBC, on BBC news about obesity, and what that was about is that they found a obesity gene, that means that patients who have this gene is more likely to have obesity, irrespective of their lifestyle. And so that's exactly what we do – we are trying to locate genes such as the obesity gene.

So that's pretty much what I do, and this is how I do it. So in a very kind of brief, simplistic view what we do is we analyse two sets of genetic data. The first set of genetic data comes from patients that carry a disease that we're interested in, so for example, obesity. The second set of genetic data comes from patients that don't carry the disease, so they are the patients, people who don't have obesity. And we analyse the two together, and hopefully what we find is that in the obesity data set, they all carry a set of genes that are not found in the other data set where people don't have obesity. So it's a very, very simple view. We are talking about huge amounts of data, and we're using statistics to kind of model, analyse this data, so that's why we're in the statistics department.

So that was how I do it. And finally why, OK, so we're doing this because by locating the genetic causes of certain diseases, we're better understanding the diseases, and eventually that will hopefully lead to a cure or at least a prevention for these diseases. So, for example, pharmaceutical companies, by knowing where the obesity gene is, will be able to develop drugs that negates the effects of this gene. So hopefully in the future there might be a drug that cures obesity or at least prevents it. And so that is why we do it.

So that's pretty much the 'what', the 'how' and the 'why'. So hopefully now you know a little bit more about mathematical genetics about what we do. I hope you have found it interesting and thank you for listening and now I am happy to take any questions.

Step 5

Good morning everyone. My name is Zhan Su. I'm a PhD student at the University of Oxford, and today I'll be telling you a little bit about my research. I will tell you a little bit about what I do, how I do it and finally why I do it. The presentation will be about five minutes. I'll be happy to take any questions you might have at the end.

So first of all, what is mathematical genetics? In mathematical genetics our main role is to identify those areas of our genome that causes disease. So let me just digress for a second. Some of you might have seen these films, the Matrix, The Terminator or iRobot. And all these films tell a story of humans against machines. After seeing these films you might also get the idea that actually humans are not that different from machines: whereas machines are made of inorganic materials such as metals, our bodies are made of organic materials such as proteins; whereas machines are designed from a blueprint, our bodies are designed from a blueprint encoded in our DNA; and finally whereas machines break down, our bodies succumb to disease. In essence our bodies are machines. And I would just like to go back to that third point that I mentioned which is machines breaking down. Machines break down because it hasn't been maintained properly, and likewise our bodies break down because we haven't been taking care of it properly. We are talking about, for example, bad diet, lack of exercise or a bad environment. But machines also break down because it hasn't been designed properly – there may be a design fault, and likewise there are design faults in our DNA, there are errors in our DNA which causes disease. So those are genetic diseases and here is a list of some of those that you might have heard of. I've highlighted obesity, because that is quite topical at the moment, and this was an article in The

Times earlier this month. And what this article is about, is that scientists found a obesity gene which means that patients who carry this gene are more likely to have obesity, irrespective of their diet, of their environment or of their exercise habits.

So that is essentially what we do, and I'm going to tell you a little bit about how we do it. To put it in very simple terms we take genetic samples from a group of patients who exhibit a disease that we're interested in. So for example a group of obese patients and we compare that genetic data to a group of patients who do not exhibit the disease, so non-obese patients. What we hope to find is that the obese patients carry a gene that the non-obese patients don't carry, and if we find that, then that kind of suggests to us that it could be a disease gene.

And finally, why would we want to do this? Well, by finding the genetic basis of diseases, it allows us to better understand the disease which will lead to a prevention and maybe even a cure. And just to finish off, this is a Times article which was actually front page news last week, and what this story says is that pharmaceutical companies hope to be able to make a pill that negates the effects of faulty genes, of disease genes, so this is, for the first time this is kind of evidence that offers us hope of a real cure, an actual cure for genetic diseases.

So this brings me to the end of my presentation. Let's just recap what we've talked about. First of all I told you what mathematical genetics is about. It's about finding those parts of our genome that causes disease. I've told you how we do it, which is to compare genetic data between patients and non-patients, and finally I've told you why we do it, which is to hopefully find a prevention and a cure for these diseases. Now you know a little bit more about my research. This is something I think will impact on all of our lives in the future. I hope you've found it interesting and thank you very much for listening.

3 Full presentation

A 🔊 5.06 Dan

– I've got a question. What do you think is the colour of the moment? What is so 'in' right now?

– Green?

– That's right. That's why we are here. We are going to talk about the green issue. And you know what? Because as you see the first page of newspaper, you see it's all about green issues at the moment, like, you know, climate changes, global warmings. That's why I'm here today and my mission is to bring a little bit of green into your lives at work, and now there are three parts that I would like to cover, and let me introduce you to my chart. Today I am going to give a green talk. My name is Dan, and the first topic I would like to talk about is, 'Why green?' So we are going to kind of step back and look at why and how important the environment is so important to our lives. And secondly we are going to talk about the agenda, the green agenda at work, at your work, your organisation, and the last one, we're going to do some kind of awareness exercise, which I think is the most important part of this presentation.

Let's come on to the first one, why green? You probably expect me to bring you some figures about the green issues like how many people are dying because of the, you know, those issues that effect by this climate change, global warming, like Katrina, but I'm not going to do that. Today I'm going to do something like, I'm going to make it more personal and I want to see this talk as to be kind of giving you awareness of what you can do to bring green issue to your life and your work. So, I'm going to tell a story instead and it's story about my friend, actually. This friend, her name is Georgina, and she's an editor in a publishing company, but we are very good friends and we often talk about everything, so what we have just talked about is the green issue, like somebody raise up the topic and ask about like, I don't get it, why like the environment is so over-valued, the environment issue is so over-talked, overvalued. And Georgina, as an environmentalist, she's also … plus a full-time editor she's also a full-time environmentalist. So she said, 'Imagine this: if the world is a person, what is the environment, do you think?'. The environment is like the health of that person. And right now, if you see the world, right now the world is like a very heavy second hand smoker. I'm sure that he's not having a good diet because all the thing was taken out. It's like if you compare the person who is in such a bad condition right now, and even though how much technologies or we advance, but if the health doesn't function properly, we can't do anything. And I think she gives the picture of how important the environment is. Like is to you, health is the first primary of life, priority of life. So I think you can see now how important is the environment.

Now let's move on to the second topic that I would like to make is about the green agenda. As a part of an organisation, I'm sure your organisation have now like a green agenda, but the question is, are you aware of that agenda, as a part of your organisation? And I did some tests, to my friend, again, to Gina, and she told me that, she told me about, you know, the green agenda in her publishing house and she said that we now use the eco-friendly printing, we now doing some kind of carbon-neutral off-setting emission. So now, in the business world even there are many people who are becoming eco-sensitive. And that's become a factor in the business world when people want to make a decision. Now green issues become important. So if as a part of this company you are aware of this issue, it's helping your company as well. So that's why today I would like to raise your awareness and we're going to do that by this exercise, which is the last one. This exercise is aimed to some kind of helping you to see everything in your life now a bit greener, so let's … I have a … I'll introduce you the green schedule. It's a list of the normal daily everyday routines, what you're going to do. So I would like have you tell me, just pick one and have you tell me what have you done during that time that is green. Like, for example, at 8am today I bought a … I went to Tesco, but I didn't take a plastic bag because I have my … shopping bag with me, so that's green. So, how about you, Svitlana?
– I'm cycling.

– Yes, that's very good, that's green travel. How about, what's your name again?
– Koa. I walk to work.
– Right. That's good. That's like cycling. How about you, Anna?
– I have a nylon shopping bag in my handbag which I use instead of getting plastic bags from supermarkets.
– How about you?
– I recycled at lunchtime, I went down and I took all the spare papers from the seminar down to the recycling.
– That's very good. And you see this morning you have done something green. Now how about this afternoon, you do another one which is green, which is a kind of helping, which is little changes, but it make a lot of difference. So that's bring me to my conclusion and the conclusion is that you know how important the environment is, but perhaps you are not aware enough that these small changes can make a difference to the world. Think of the Georgina world in that the world is another person and now he needs some help, he needs some cure, and the cure is your care for the environment … that's my presentation. Thank you very much.

B Yale 12: And **you** know what? / Because as **you** see the first page of newspaper / **health** is the first primary of life, priority of life
Common power words: **Imagine** this
Simile: The environment is **like** the health of that person / right now the world is **like** a very heavy second hand smoker.
Metaphor and analogy: The world is another person and now / he needs some help, he needs some cure, and the cure is your care for the environment
Storytelling: So, I'm going to **tell a story** instead and it's story about my friend (Dan came back to the story and his relationship with his friend as a theme in the presentation)
Self disclosure: I'm going to make it more personal / but we are very good friends and we often talk about everything (Dan came back to the story and his relationship with his friend as a theme in the presentation)

C 5.07 Svitlana
Good afternoon ladies and gentlemen. My name is Svitlana. I'm delighted to be here with you today. The goal of my presentation is to tell you how we can save our planet by recycling more and more, more and more. As Richard Burke said once, 'If you want to have things that you have never had before, you need to start doing things that you have never done before.' And that apply to all of us. Either we already recycling champions or just considering the possibility of recycling, there is always a way to recycle more and more, more and more. I will tell you the elephant story. If you have ever been to a circus or zoo, you have probably wondered why it is that the huge, old elephants and tiny baby elephants tethered with exactly the same chain. A

fully grown-up elephant could, if it wanted to, simply walk away without even breaking into a sweat. But, that's just the point. The old elephant has forgotten what it is like to struggle, to be free. The baby elephant, who constantly pulls and tugs at the chain, still has the motivation to succeed. That's the end of the story. So, let's be the baby elephants and struggle for the better environment.

Today, firstly, we will discuss the importance of recycling in saving our planet and postponing the greenhouse effect. Secondly, I will brief you on the current situation on the global warming. And thirdly, I will give you some ideas on increasing recycling because, as I said before, there are always ways to recycle more and more, more and more. My presentation will take approximately five minutes and I will be happy to answer your questions at the end of my presentation.

So, let's start then. I will start by telling you what the greenhouse effect is. So, the greenhouse effect is a process by which absorption and emission of infrared radiation by atmospheric gases warms a planet's atmosphere and surface. Sounds hot, doesn't it? On earth, the major natural greenhouse gases are water vapour which causes about thirty-six to seventy percent of greenhouse effects. It's also carbon dioxide, nine to twenty-six percent of greenhouse effects. Methane four to nine percent greenhouse effects, and ozone, three to seven percent of greenhouse effect. The atmospheric concentration of carbon dioxide, and methane have increased by thirty-one and one hundred forty-nine percent respectively, above pre-industrial levels since seventeen fifteen. This is considerably higher than at any time during the last six hundred fifty thousand years, the period for which reliable data has been extracted from ice cores. Pretty scary picture, isn't it? And we need – and can – change it. How do we do that? I will tell you five things you can do to reduce the global warming. Please remember, it's not very difficult and we all can do it. First thing, reduce, re-use, recycle. I will open it for you. Do your part to reduce waste by choosing re-usable products instead of disposables? Buying products with minimal packaging will help to reduce waste, and whenever you can, recycle paper, plastic, newspaper, glass and aluminium cans. If there is not a recycling programme at your workplace or in your community, ask about starting one.

Let's go to my second point. Second point: change a light bulb. Wherever practical, replace regular light bulbs with compact, fluorescent light bulbs. Fluorescent light bulbs last ten times longer than incandescent bulbs, use two thirds less energy, and give off seventy percent less heat.

Let's move to the third point. The third point is: buy energy-efficient products. When it is time to buy a new car, choose one that offers good gas mileage. Home appliances now come in a range of energy-efficient models and compact fluorescent bulbs are designed to provide more natural looking light, while using far less energy than standard light bulbs.

Let's go to the fourth point. So the fourth point is: use the off switch. Save electricity and reduce global warming by turning off lights when you leave a room and using only as much light as you need. And remember to turn off your television, video player, stereo and computer when you are not using them. It is also a good idea to turn off the water when you are not using it. While brushing your teeth, shampooing the dog, or washing your car, turn off the water until you really need it for instance. You will reduce your water bill and help to conserve a vital resource.

Let's go to the fifth point. The fifth point is: plant a tree. If you have the means to plant a tree, start digging. During photosynthesis, trees and other plants absorb carbon dioxide and give off oxygen. They're an integral part of the natural atmospheric exchange cycle here on earth. But there are too few of them to fully counter the increases in carbon dioxide, caused by automobile traffic, manufacturing and other human activities. A single tree will absorb approximately one ton of carbon dioxide during its lifetime. You see, it does not cost you a lot to save the earth. It even costs you less if you become an efficient user of the resources provided to us by mother earth. Common sense also helps.

Let's recap on these five points. First one: reduce, re-use, recycle. Second one: change a light bulb. Thirdly, buy energy efficient products. Fourth one: use the off switch and fifth one: plant a tree.

That brings me to a conclusion that recognises the importance of the fight against global warming and taking reasonable steps to slow it down, we can actually improve a lot our life, and most definitely the lives of our children. According to a survey in this week's Time Magazine, eighty-five percent of Americans think global warming is happening. The other fifteen percent work for the White House. Blame Giuliani for this joke, but be aware of global warming. Can you say 'yes'?

– Yes.

– Thank you for agreeing with me that recycling is really, really important. One thing to remember: save the world. Recycle, recycle, recycle. Thank you very much for your time and I am happy to take your questions now.

4 The main advantage of working with a script is that a script can help in the learning process as you experiment with different techniques and language. The more you practise the better you get. There is also an argument that a script is useful for certain kinds of presentation, e.g. a lecture. However, there is probably a point in the learning process where presenters need to work less with a script in order to connect with the audience. Dan's audience felt that Dan had improved his presentation style immensely by Step 5 and that he had 'found his voice'. Svitlana relied on a script throughout the training. This enabled her to integrate many new techniques but she needed to take a further step by presenting without the aid of a script. This may have enabled her to pace the presentation and connect with the audience better.

Step 6 Love your audience ... not everyone is like you

1 Something for everyone

Left and right brain

A

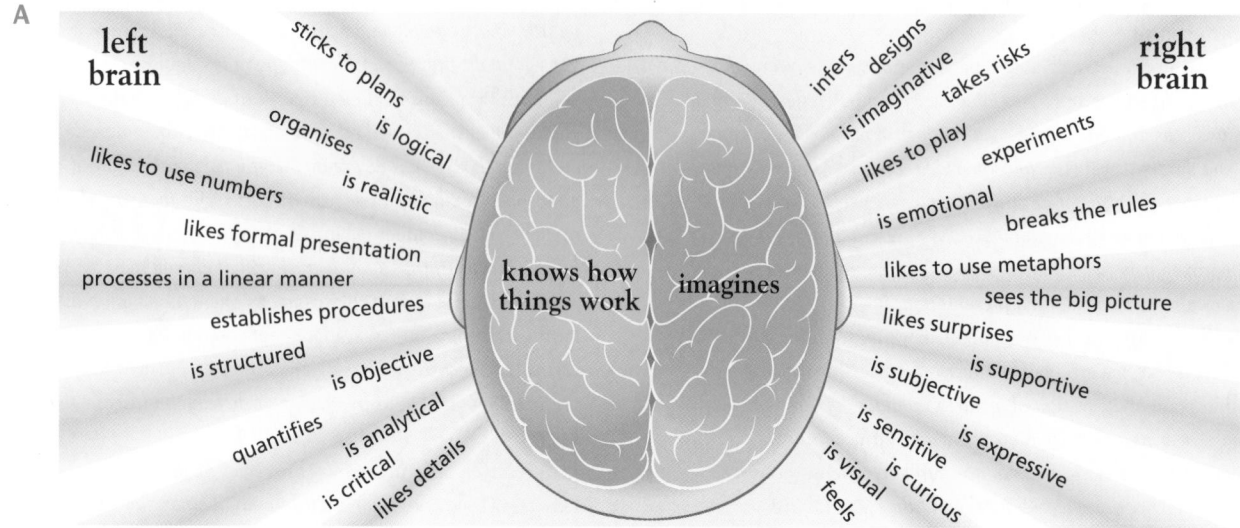

B
Step 1	Left
Step 2	Right
Step 3	Left
Step 4	Left
Step 5	Right

Representational systems

A

1	Visual	14	Gustatory
2	Kinaesthetic	15	Kinaesthetic
3	Visual	16	Auditory
4	Gustatory	17	Visual
5	Olfactory	18	Olfactory
6	Auditory	19	Auditory
7	Visual	20	Visual
8	Olfactory	21	Auditory
9	Visual	22	Visual
10	Kinaesthetic	23	Auditory
11	Olfactory	24	Visual
12	Visual	25	Kinaesthetic
13	Auditory		

B 🔘 **6.01 Zhan**

When you sit in the car, you notice how soft and supportive the seats are. You can adjust them to make them even more comfortable for you, and as you sink in, you will notice a smell of real leather. Take a deep breath and start driving. You will notice how quiet the car is. Apart from a soft murmur and a gentle hum, you don't hear very much at all. The car gleams. It looks compact and tidy. It has been designed to make the best use of space. It is a lovely thing to look at.

1	soft	8	hum
2	supportive	9	hear
3	comfortable	10	gleams
4	smell	11	looks
5	breath	12	space
6	quiet	13	look
7	murmur		

C
1	K	6	A	11	V
2	K	7	A	12	V
3	K	8	A	13	V
4	O	9	A		
5	O / K	10	V		

Multiple intelligences

B
a	1	k	5
b	1	l	2
c	4 and / or 5	m	2
d	3	n	2
e	2 and / or 4	o	3
f	4	p	5
g	3	q	1 and / or 5
h	6	r	7
i	6	s	4
j	1, 2, 3, 4, 6, 7 (depends on the nature and subject matter of the film)		

Personality types

A The Myers-Briggs Type Indicator is a psychometric instrument based on the theories of Carl Jung's psychological types. It does not assess intelligence or aptitude. According to Jungian theory, individuals are born with a predisposition for certain personality preferences. There is no 'best' preference and all preferences are equally valid and important.

MBTI identifies basic preferences:
Extraverted or **I**ntroverted: Do you prefer to focus on the outer world or on your own inner world?
Sensing or i**N**tuitive: Do you prefer to focus on the basic information you take in or do you prefer to interpret and add meaning?
Thinking or **F**eeling: When making decisions, do you prefer to first look at logic and consistency or first look at the people and special circumstances?
Judging or **P**erceiving: In dealing with the outside world, do you prefer to get things decided or do you prefer to stay open to new information and options?

and identifies and describes sixteen four-letter personality types:

ISTJ	ISFJ	INFJ	INTJ
ISTP	ISFP	INFP	INTP
ESTP	ESFP	ENFP	ENTP
ESTJ	ESFJ	ENFJ	ENTJ

Suggestion
3 All these types exist and there will be a number of different types in any audience. Not everyone is like you and considering other types is a useful strategy in preparing a presentation.

C a (8) Perceiving Types
  b (3) Sensing Types
  c (7) Judging Types
  d (5) Thinking Types
  e (1) Extraverts
  f (6) Feeling Types
  g (4) Intuitive Types
  h (2) Introverts

D 6.02 **Zhan and César**
– *Good afternoon everyone. Very welcome to our presentation. My colleague, Zhan Su and I will be telling you how to improve your life in five minutes by doing something very, very simple. So the first question I'm going to ask you is, 'Do you drive a*

car like this? If the answer is 'yes', then let me ask you the next question. 'Would you like to have more respect, more money and more success in your life?' I assume the answer is 'yes'. So my colleague will tell you exactly how to do it and what to do.
– All right, gentlemen, this is what you need. A BMW. Oh yeah! OK, this machine is a remarkable car and it will bring you success. First of all let me just read to you what it is like to drive. When you sit in the car, you notice how soft and supportive the seats are. You can adjust them to make them even more comfortable for you, and as you sink in, you will notice a smell of real leather. Take a deep breath and start driving. You will notice how quiet the car is. Apart from a soft murmur and a gentle hum, you don't hear very much at all. The car gleams. It looks compact and tidy. It has been designed to make the best use of space. It is a lovely thing to look at. Not only that, gentlemen – a BMW has been proven to bring you success, and here are some statistics for you to look at. A BMW brings you more money, a better role in your company, makes you sexier to women and for those environmentally conscious ones of you, it will make you a greener person. So just to conclude, we've told you a very simple way to improve your life, to bring success to your life. So go out there and do it today. Buy a BMW. Thank you for listening.

Suggestions
Perceiving (give time for decision)
Sensing (clear, practical, facts and evidence)
Judging (clear plan and structure)
Thinking (clear, precise, complete argument)
Feeling (human benefits and happiness)
Intuitive (the big picture)

Find Your Voice
Suggestions for resources

Pictures	Literature
Newspaper articles	Books on presentations
Headlines	Stories in books
Posters	Stories in my organisation
Cartoons	Podcasts
Video & DVD	Personal ideas and thoughts
Objects	Shocking statements
Other presentations	New vocabulary
TV	Internet
Statistics	Puzzles
Games	Quotations

2 **Full presentation**

A 6.03 **Svitlana and Dan**
– *Hello, hello, hello everybody. My name is Svitlana.*
– *And my name is Dan and today we are going to learn to trust each other. Do you trust your colleagues?*
– *Yes? No?*
– *Do you want to learn to trust them more?*
– *And that's what we are here for.*

– Now I will tell you about the benefits of, you know, learning to trust each other, but what I will tell you is the problem and the disadvantages at work, that might occur when you don't trust your colleagues. Imagine when you are very hardworking person, you become over-loaded with work because you don't learn to trust, to share your work with your colleagues, and that's the first problem.

– That's why we've brought you today the best kept secret of trust. It's an incredibly easy, but very efficient exercise. You will love it. So here it is, the hottest, the sexiest, the most fantastic exercise of all. Lie down on the floor, Dan.

– Are you sure you want me to do that?

– I'm sure I do.

– OK. I will learn to trust you.

– Jump. Jump. Jump. Jump. Jump. Jump. Jump. Jump. How do you feel, Dan?

– Oh, I feel more confident in you now Svitlana, and that's the thing that I want to point … and that brings me to the point that I want to make about the benefits of learning to trust someone else is, it's all about confidence in yourself and others and when that happens, the workflow will be much better.

– And it keeps you fit as well.

– Sorry. Are you still want for more evidence?

– Look at us. To summarise, we need to trust each other more, and to conclude:

– I will recommend you to practise this exercise on every Monday, before you go to work … before you start working, and by Friday you will see the difference in the way you learn to trust your colleagues, and the way you work. And that's only better because now you will have much more confidence in your colleagues. Thank you. She just got me a pen.

– No more sexual harassment, no more misunderstandings, no more anxiety at work, and …

– Trust us, it's all about trust.

Step 7 Questions are a big opportunity, aren't they?

1 Questions

Introduction

A 1 There are a number of reasons. It could be simply to clarify, to get more information or to elaborate on a point. Hidden agendas can include 'testing' the presenter or introducing new dimensions to the topic area. Some may ask a question just for the sake of asking a question.

2 The presenter creates a relationship with the audience and clarifies meaning and misunderstandings. Dialogue can be a much more comfortable style for some presenters, even when they are speaking another language.

3 The presenter can lose structure or go completely off the point, overshooting timings and deadlines for the presentation. He / She can forget to include important points of the presentation and may lose the impact of the final message.

4 This depends on personal presentation style and the type of presentation. See the suggestions in the text.

Reporting questions
Grammar: Indirect questions

B 1 what the accident rate was last year.
2 why I responded in that way.
3 how many clients we handled last year.
4 if / whether we foresee any change in the situation.
5 if / whether the market can sustain this growth rate.
6 what our pricing structure is.
7 if / whether we've had any experience of this with other clients.
8 exactly when the auditors came.

Paraphrasing

C **Suggestions**

Note: The suggested answers below focus on putting a more positive spin on potentially negative questions.

So you're asking about:
1 how we've planned for such a problem next time.
2 our credentials.
3 my reasons for advocating this.
4 the minor drawbacks.
5 our pricing strategy.
6 our credentials.
7 the approved budget.
8 the methodology we used.

2 Answers
Answering strategies

A 1 c   2 b   3 b   4 a   5 b   6 a   7 c   8 b

Notes on answers
1 **Q:** The questioner is asking for clarification.
A: The presenter listens to the question and paraphrases / clarifies. He / She uses the following phrase to introduce the clarification: *Let me put it in another way, …* Other similar phrases include:
Let me go over it again.
What I would like to say is …
It is also advisable to check the clarification, by asking, for example:
Does that make the point clearer?
Does that answer the question?
Have I made that clearer?

2 **Q:** The questioner asks a sequence of questions.

A: It's important to remember that the presenter isn't responsible for a stream of (maybe illogical) thinking from the questioner, especially when presenting in another language.

The presenter listens to the complete sequence and answers the sequence by breaking it down into single questions.

He / She makes it clear the questioner has asked more than one question.

Alternative strategies:

1 Paraphrase the easiest question in the sequence first. Answer this question. Paraphrase the next question and answer this question.

2 Paraphrase the easiest question in the sequence only. This also gives you the opportunity to avoid difficult or irrelevant questions.

Check with the questioner that the question is answered by using one of these phrases:

OK?

Does that answer your question?

Does that clarify this?

3 **Q:** The question isn't a question but a statement.

A: The presenter listens to the statement. He / She gives the statement as a positive paraphrase and then answers this paraphrasing.

4 **Q:** The questioner expresses emotion, makes a statement and uses negative vocabulary.

A: The presenter listens to each part of the question. He / She paraphrases, using more positive vocabulary and without addressing the emotion and then answers this paraphrasing.

5 **Q:** The questioner is asking the presenter to agree with him / her. It's possible that the underlying intention of the question is not to do with the second option.

A: The presenter listens, paraphrases using more positive vocabulary and answers the paraphrasing.

He / She does not paraphrase the request for agreement and does not answer with 'yes' or 'no'.

6 **Q:** The questioner asks about a point that is coming later in the presentation.

A: The presenter listens, but doesn't answer the question. He / She refers the question forward to a later point in the presentation, demonstrating effective management of the questions and presentation.

7 **Q:** The question is not about the presenter's area of expertise.

A: The presenter listens and refers the question to the person in the room who is best qualified to answer the question.

Alternative strategies:

1 Check the information and send it after the presentation. This can be a delaying strategy and gives the presenter thinking time.

That's not actually in the scope of this presentation. But I can check it and get back to you.

2 State that you don't know. You can't be an expert in every area and don't need to put unnecessary pressure on yourself when a question is beyond the scope of the presentation or your field of business.

I'm afraid I don't know the answer to that question.

I'm afraid I can't answer that question.

8 **Q:** The questioner is using words that the presenter doesn't understand.

A: The presenter asks the questioner for clarification. This is a useful strategy if the presenter is a non-native speaker as it can give thinking time or even help avoid a question.

When you say … do you mean …?

I didn't get that. Could you repeat your question?

I'm very sorry but I don't understand.

Q&A analysis

A 7.01

1 **Q:** *Are we talking about the whole of Ukraine here? How many people are we going to train?*

Svitlana: *Thank you very much for your question So, you're asking how many people we're going to train. We're …*

2 **Q:** *So, what does a person normally earn in Ukraine?*

Svitlana: *You're asking what is the salary of average person in Ukraine. It's a very low salary. But, we're not speaking about ordinary people …*

3 **Q:** *Could you tell us a little bit more about the kind of training that you're envisaging giving these people? And how it would benefit companies?*

Svitlana: *Your question is about how … what is the training we are going to provide to these specialists and how the companies would benefit. Let me take your question in two parts. So, the first question is what is the training about. This training will be provided by a very well-recognised company in Germany … And, let me come back to your second question, how the companies would benefit. The thing you do, the companies would pay only £100,000 which I believe you will agree with me is not a very big amount for such a big company, but after that you can have as many specialists as you want.*

4 **Q:** *I was wondering how are you going to convince these people to work for half a salary?*

Svitlana: *Thank you for your question. Your question is about why would these people agree to work for half a salary.*

5 Q: *So, in your opinion, how many genes cause disease?*
Zhan: *How many genes cause disease. Well, that's a very good question and it's also a very difficult question to answer because the answer is we don't know.*

6 Q: *I've got a question. How do you know a gene is a disease gene?*
Zhan: *How do we know a gene is a disease gene. Well, as I say, after this analysis we have a list of candidate genes that could be a disease gene. We then send off these results to biologists who will confirm our findings.*

7 Q: *Can I just ask a question about these pills? I mean, are they expensive to produce? Are they likely to be available to everybody who has this kind of genetic gene?*
Zhan: *Right. So, first of all, are they expensive to produce. Well, I'm afraid I'm just involved in discovering these disease genes. So, this is something that the pharmaceutical companies will have to come up with and, I'm afraid that I can't answer that question. The second part of the question is … sorry, remind me, what is the second part of your question?*

8 Q: *If I understand you correctly, you're promoting IP as a positive thing to teach in schools. But, what are the negative effects?*
César: *So, the question is the negative effects of IP teaching in schools. Well, I'm glad you asked the question because it's a very interesting question, but at the same time it's a bit – I would say – highly topical at the moment. It's more to do with the philosophy of IP.*

9 Q: *That was my question actually. I understand … How can we finance this? The extra cost?*
César: *So, the question is budget.*

10 Q: *So, are you saying that teaching IP is a good thing?*
César: *If I understand you correctly, you're saying if I am advocating the positive things of IP. I haven't actually got to that point. I think at this stage I'm actually giving you the facts. I'm actually giving you the whole picture. I'm going to come down to that point later on. So, if you could just hold onto that, I would really appreciate it.*
Note César should have said:
… you're asking if I am advocating the positive things of IP not
(*… you're ~~saying~~ if I am advocating the positive things of IP.*)
If you could just hold onto that point for a moment, I'll be coming to it later on is more natural English than *I'm going to come down to that point later on. If you can just hold onto that.*
He may have confused the meaning of *actually* which does not mean 'now' or 'at the moment' in English.

B 1 c 3 f 5 a 7 b 9 j
     2 g 4 d 6 e 8 i 10 h

Hidden meanings

A Note that analysis can also depend on the relationship between the questioner and presenter, the context and the tone of voice.

Suggestions
1 A statement
2 A statement followed by question. Uses negative vocabulary. Emotional phrasing.
3 An emotional statement – not a question. Needs clarification. What is the question exactly?
4 An emotional statement followed by question.
5 A sequence of questions with a statement in the middle.
6 A request for agreement with questioner.
7 A request for agreement / an emotional statement / testing the presenter. Needs clarification.
8 Emotional? Is the question the price or the presenter's credentials or credibility? Needs clarification.
9 Negative vocabulary. Is this a request for clarification or a question about price? Needs clarification.
10 Is this related to the presentation and does it need an answer? Is this a question about credentials or price?
11 Negative vocabulary. A question about the graphic company's credentials and not about 'justification'.
12 A request for agreement with speaker. Emotional?
13 A request for clarification.
14 A question followed by an emotional statement. Address the question.

B a 10   d 12   g 7   j 11   m 2
    b 1   e 3   h 9   k 13   n 6
    c 14   f 5   i 8   l 4

7.02 César

Good morning everyone. Welcome to my presentation. I'm very happy to be here. And I'll be talking to you about introducing IP to our law curriculum, and I will be highlighting the most important points to be considered in order to introduce this subject in our law faculty. And, please feel free to ask any questions at any time, all right? So, before I actually start, let me show you some staggering figures about intellectual property. The first point is ninety percent of all international law firms in our country have an IP department. This is something absolutely staggering. The second point is that eighty percent of all newspapers and magazines discuss IP related stories on an everyday basis. So no day goes by without having an IP related story in our newspaper. And a third point is that eighty percent of all international agreements have IP provisions, so this is a fact, and I believe is absolutely staggering.
So my presentation will be divided into three main points. The main point will be the subject matter, so I will be talking about what IP is all about and what it all includes. In the second point I would like

to talk about why IP is relevant, and why we should introduce it to our law curriculum, and why our students should study the subject while doing law at university. And finally, in my third point, I will be discussing how we can actually organise an IP course without incurring very high costs, and without having to introduce or having to bring in more resources, human resources or facilities to the faculty.

So moving on to my first point: the subject matter is intellectual property or IP as many people call it. And the core subject will be copyright, patent and trademarks. These core subjects is always complemented by secondary areas such as trade secrets, designs and data bases. Very briefly, let me just say to you that copyright is mainly concerned with the production and the protection of creative works, such as books, films, performance rights, for example, etc. And it is mainly related to artistic works. As far as patents are concerned, let me just say to you that that's actually related to inventions such as, for example, patenting DNA or the creation of pharmaceuticals or the invention of a new method to produce a particular product, etc. And trademarks are mainly trade indentificators that traders use in commerce to identify and distinguish their goods. And as far as trade secrets, designs and data bases are concerned, they are not really relevant, but they complement the core subjects. Let me just say to you that trade secrets are normally concerned with the protection of ideas and particular methods of doing things in the workplace, whereas designs are normally concerned with the protection of particular industrial designs that traders use in commerce and data bases are normally concerned with the creation and protection of compilations of data that some scientists or some companies normally undertake.

– If I understand you correctly, you are promoting that IP is a positive thing to teach in schools. But what are the negative effects?

– So the question is the negative effects of IP teaching in schools. Well, I'm glad you asked the question, because it's a very interesting question, but at the same time a bit, I would say, highly topical at the moment. It's more to do with philosophy of IP, and as far as I am concerned, much paper has been devoted to the physical … to the philosophical explanation of IP and its pros and cons, but as far as I can see for every argument we mount in favour of IP, there will always be another argument against it, so I would say it is more to do with the balance – how far we want to go and how much protection we want to give, so I'm afraid I would not have a definite answer for your question.

So, moving on to my next aspect of my presentation, the why IP is relevant. I've highlighted two main points in this part. The first one is what IP seeks to promote, and the second one is the underlying principles, the over-riding principles that support the whole area of IP, and on this point, let me just say three main things. Intellectual property promotes, or seeks to promote the works of the arts, the investment and research in technological advances for example in medicine, science, etc. And market efficiency normally achieved by trademark law. And, on the other hand, intellectual property has a very strong, solid basis, and I would summarise these three basic

principles in this three ways. The first is the eighth commandment which most of us I am sure recognise and it's 'thou shalt not steal'. And that is a very basic underlying principle that is also present, and is also very common in our legal system. So if I produce a piece of work … yes …

– So, are you saying that teaching IP is a good thing?

– If I understand you correctly, you're saying if I am advocating the positive things of IP. I haven't actually got to that point. I think at this stage I'm actually giving you the facts. I'm actually giving you the whole picture. I'm going to come down to that point later on, so if you could just hold on to that, I'd really appreciate it.

So as I was discussing, the first underlying principle of IP is that thou shalt not steal. If I produce a piece of work, or if I create a particular invention, I have every right to retain and to recoup some sort of – this is going to bring me down to my third point – that if I produce a piece of work, we cannot see any principle or any logic as to why you should take it from me when I have produced it. And this first principle is actually interlinked with the underlying principle which is 'sweat of the brow'. And when we talk about 'sweat of the brow' we talk about the effort that a creator, a writer, an author puts into a particular work. That effort, that brings me down to my third point, should be rewarded. So if I create a piece of work, we cannot see the reason why someone else should take it, without my permission, and rather than … not giving any protection, we should actually be encouraging people to produce work by rewarding them, by assuring them that something they produce will be protected.

So much about the relevance of IP. Let me move on to my next point … yes …

– So, what's the public's gain?

– So the question is what the public actually gains by us giving IP protection? That's a two-fold question, which is easy to answer in one … let me just talk about the positive things about IP. So when we talk about IP, we talk about promoting works of art, promoting the creation and dissemination of books, for example, the creation, invention and research investments and all the rest of it. What the public gains is basically more knowledge, dissemination of culture, dissemination of knowledge, and more available resources, right? At the same time, here comes the downside to IP; IP imposes some sort of fetter on competition. Because you are creating … you are creating a particular piece of work, you also gain a monopoly to stop others from using your work. So let's say that it's inherent in IP, some sorts of limitation on the use that others can use of your work, but we cannot see other way of encouraging people to produce and at the same time rewarding them for what they do. Obviously this comes at a price. What we're trying to do with IP is to strike a happy balance between the work of creators and the public access to these works.

So finally, let me just address the organisation of the course. And on this point I would like to talk about the teaching and the course itself and who may be qualified or best qualified to teach the course. So let me just say that teaching can ideally take place either yearly or by semesters, and I would be more in favour of teaching the subject over the course of a year, because then we cover more aspects of IP and we give students more time to think about it and to take in all the information they study. And secondly, I believe understanding IP is far more effective once our students have studied our core subjects such as tort and civil law. And I would say they normally go hand-in-hand, and I can't see any reason why they shouldn't be able to understand the subject very clearly once they've done these two main courses. And thirdly our faculty boasts a really good number of intellectual property and commercial lawyers, so I believe these two groups of lawyers, these two groups of teachers and fellows could easily undertake the teaching and that would be a very nice partnership. So, in terms of resources … yes …

– That was my question actually. I understand that, I mean … how can we finance this, the extra cost?

– So the question is budget. I don't envisage any major investment in human resources, to be honest. I believe that the resources the faculty has at the minute are sufficient to cover the costs of the course and I cannot see any disruption in our budgetary finances.

So, to cap it all, let me just summarise the points I have discussed, and we've looked at what the subject matter is, we covered six different areas of IP, then we moved on to the relevance of IP and its underlying principles, and finally we looked at who could teach the subject and how, without actually allocating so much financial resources or human resources, we can actually teach the course and join the band wagon of IP teaching across the world. So I really trust that I have given you a very clear insight into the feasibility and availability of intellectual property courses at faculties and I am very happy to take any questions if you have any. So thank you very much for listening.

7.03

Svitlana: I'm just so happy I was chosen as a candidate to do it because I gained so, so much out of it. I can't say I don't have the words to describe it, because I learnt a lot of new words, I learnt a lot of new techniques and I just feel so much more confident. Just amazing. The one that I really love and the one which is very easy to use for me and which comes out naturally is the Rule of Three, when you repeat something three times, three times, three times. When you say it once, they think, did she say it? When you say it twice, they say, oh probably she said it, and when you say it three times, they know for sure that you mean it so that's why it's very important. And structure, actually, I mean, structurising the presentation, it makes such a big difference. And recently I had a very short presentation in a small community and everybody was doing their presentation sitting down, and I just stood up and it was very spontaneous but the way I did it everybody was very impressed and I thought, oh well and I wouldn't have thought to it, and I wouldn't have structured it this way and I would not have done this and this if I would not have come on this course. So I am really, really grateful to all the people with who I work and our coach, I mean she was just amazing. If I would to describe it into words, I would repeat one word three times: brilliant, brilliant, brilliant.

Dan: After I finish the course I feel that I have learnt so many things and I think it's really helping in my process of both preparing the presentation and doing the presentation. Because I … learn many structures and techniques that can really be used in the real life. I suppose that I am like a kind of a different kind of presentation that I have achieved, you know, during … this course I learnt to do many different kinds of presentations. Now I know how to put the story into this presentation, and how to tell the story, how to make formal speeches. I think it's really useful for my job and for my everyday life. I think that the presentation that I'm going to do right after this course is going to happen next week, and I'm really looking forward to it. I feel more confident now than before. Like before it was probably oh not a presentation, now it's like OK, what should I do with it? What structure should I make for this presentation? It's kind of helping me a lot. It's for my studies, so I think I'm going to surprise my colleagues, my classmates, yeah.

Zhan: I feel the course has been very useful. It's formalised some of the things, it's formalised my preparation for presentations in the future. It's been really tiring but at the same time, I've learnt a lot. The one thing I will definitely take away with me after this course is structure in presentations and doing these signposts, so basically you are just breaking down the presentation into smaller bits so that it's easier to digest by the audience. I think my biggest challenge was perhaps taking my time in the presentation. I think I have a tendency to talk very fast, especially when I'm nervous. I kind of waffle, and I think that is still something I need to work on, just when I have kind of got a little bit lost in the presentation, I need to kind of slow down, rather than speed up, and stop waffling. I think the thing that most pleased me through the course was probably my final individual presentation, because that that was kind of built on from my first presentation that I did, the simplest presentation without all these analogies and visual aids and I think it was nice because I felt that there was a much improved presentation and it was something that was a lot more effective and a lot easier for the lay audience to understand.

César: Having finished the course just now, it's a really good feeling and I suppose it's a feeling of satisfaction because I feel like I actually, everyone did a very good job. And at the same time it is a feeling of, it's a very positive realisation in the sense that I was actually able to realise that I could do things I never thought I could, and that there is a way of doing, in this case presentations, in a very effective way, and in a very concise, brief and … I don't know, just very, very effective. So I suppose it's … a feeling of satisfaction and very positive realisation. I suppose the technique that most … that I found I could actually identify myself with more strongly was, I suppose, doing the signposting thing. Signing when I was actually going to talk about a particular thing and when I was moving onto the next. I suppose also pausing, pausing a bit, emphasising certain things and just by doing mere repetition like mantra, for example. And one thing which I never thought I could actually achieve was to be able to have a positive, or very effective, jump start to engage my audience and then start to address the topic. I thought that was a very, very good thing and, you know, very positive thing.